I0707353

SLEEP IMPROVEMENT TECHNIQUES

DAVID SANDUA

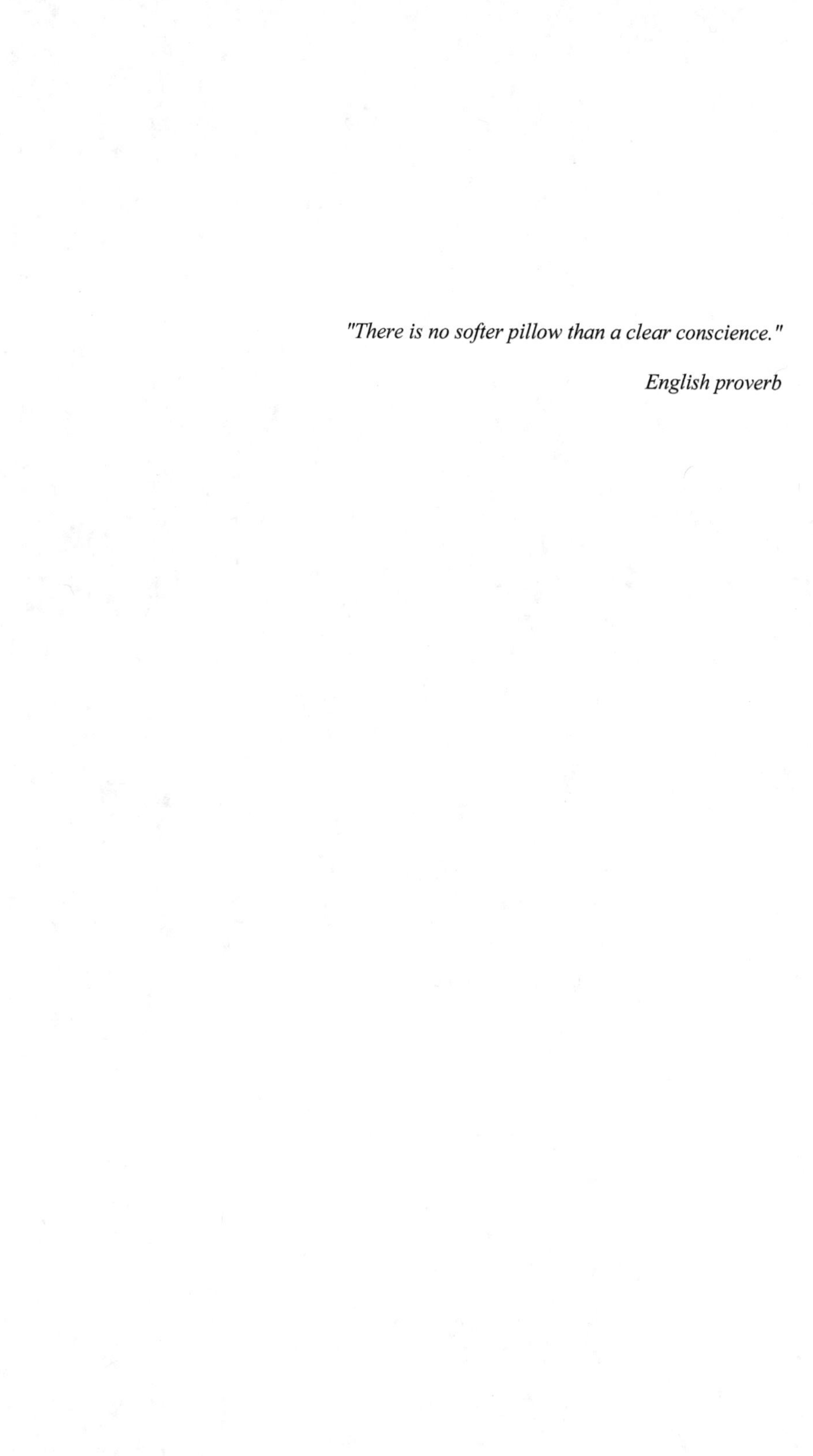

"There is no softer pillow than a clear conscience."

English proverb

ÍNDEX

INTRODUCTION

Many people struggle to get a good night's rest In today's fast-paced society due to various factors such as stress technology use and poor sleep habits. The importance of a good night's sleep is not overstated as it plays a crucial role in both physical and mental health. Sleep is essential for cognitive function emotional well-being and overall quality of life. In this essay we will explore different techniques and strategies that can help improve sleep quality and promote better overall health and wellness. Then individual can take proactive steps towards getting the restful sleep they need for life to thrive.

IMPORTANCE OF SLEEP FOR HEALTH AND WELL-BEING

An adequate amount of sleep per night is One of the most crucial components for maintaining overall health and well-being. Sleep plays a crucial role in both physical and mental health affecting everything from immunity to emotion regulation. Chronic lack of sleep increases the risk for numerous health problems including cardiovascular disease and diabetes. Sleep is also essential for cognitive function memory consolidation and mood regulation. With modern life demands it can be tempting to sacrifice sleep in favor of productivity or entertainment but if you want rest to prioritize in your life it is crucial for all to stay healthy. The patient should establish a routine sleep schedule create a relaxing bedtime routine limit screen time before bed and ensure their sleep environment is conducive to rest. By taking proactive steps to prioritize sleep individuals can improve their overall health and well-being.

PREVALENCE OF SLEEP DISORDERS AND POOR SLEEP HABITS

In today's society the prevalence of sleep disorders and unhealthy sleep habits remains a significant issue Despite the well-documented evidence of the negative impacts of poor sleep habits on overall health and well-being. About 50 to 70 million Americans suffer from some form of Sleep disorder such as Sleep apnea or insomnia According to the National Sleep foundation. In the wake of a 2017 Sleep Health study nearly one-third of Americans report getting less than the recommended seven hours of Sleep per night. These statistics highlight the widespread nature of this problem and highlight the need for effective strategies to improve sleep quality and duration.

OVERVIEW OF SLEEP IMPROVEMENT TECHNIQUES

There are various ways to improve sleep quality and duration. A common strategy is establishing a regular sleep schedule going to bed and wake up each day at the same time even on weekends. This helps regulate the body's internal clock and can lead to better sleep overall. Another technique is creating a relaxing bedtime routine such as reading a book or taking a warm bath to signal the body that it is time to rest. In addition practicing meditation or deep breathing can help reduce stress and anxiety that may interfere with falling asleep. A comfortable sleep environment can also improve sleep quality. Lastly limiting screen time before bed and avoiding caffeine and heavy meals near bedtime can also contribute to better sleep. A combination of these techniques can help individuals attain a more restful and rejuvenating night's sleep.

UNDERSTANDING SLEEP

Besides understanding the various stages of sleep it is important to also recognize the factors that affect the quality of sleep. Maintaining a consistent sleep schedule creating a calm bedtime routine and reducing exposure to screens before bed are all key practices in creating a healthy sleep environment. In addition relaxing techniques such as meditation or deep breathing exercises can help calm the mind and body before falling asleep. It is also important to consider the impact of diet and exercise on sleep quality as consuming stimulants such as caffeine late in the day or engaging in intense physical activity near bedtime can disrupt the body's natural sleep-wake cycle. By incorporating these strategies into one's daily routine individuals can improve their overall sleep hygiene and enjoy more sleepy and rejuvenating nights.

STAGES OF SLEEP AND THEIR SIGNIFICANCE

The sleep stages play a crucial role in maintaining general health and well-being. There are five stages of sleep stages with stages 1-4 which constitute non-rapid eye movement (NREM) sleep and the fifth stage being rapid eye movement (REM) sleep. Each stage serves a specific purpose in the sleep cycle with REM sleep being particularly important for memory function and cognitive function. Stages 3 and 4 are considered to be the deepest Stages of sleep where the body repairs and regenerates tissues muscles and organs. Understanding the significance of each stage is essential in developing effective sleep improvement techniques as disruptions in any stage can lead to negative consequences for the health of the individual. By putting all phases of sleep in a priority order and By finding ways to improve the quality and duration of each stage individuals can experience better physical and mental health outcomes.

CIRCADIAN RHYTHMS AND THEIR IMPACT ON SLEEP

Circadian rhythms play a crucial role in controlling sleep and wake cycle. These internal rhythms are controlled by a small region called suprachiasmatic nucleus in the brain which responds to external stimuli such as light and darkness. When our circadian rhythms are disrupted it can lead to difficulties in falling asleep or staying asleep and in poor sleep quality. Understanding our sleep schedules can greatly improve our sleep health. Proper sleep hygiene practices such as avoiding screen screens before bedtime and exposing ourselves to natural light during the day can help synchronize our circadian rhythms and promote better sleep. We can optimize our sleep patterns and experience the many benefits of a well-rested body and mind By incorporating these techniques into our daily routines.

CONSEQUENCES OF SLEEP DEPRIVATION

One of the most alarming consequences of sleep deprivation is its impact on cognition. Studies have found that lack of sleep can affect cognitive ability such as attention memory and decision-making. This can have serious implications for college students who need to perform academically well. A lack of sleep can lead to difficulties in class concentrating information and staying motivated to complete assignments. Sleep deprivation is also associated with an increased risk of depression and anxiety which can further hinder a student's ability to succeed in academic pursuits. In order to mitigate these negative consequences college students must prioritize their sleep and implement effective sleep improvement techniques.

SLEEP HYGIENE FUNDAMENTALS

For good sleeping habits and good general health. Some basic principles of sleep hygiene include maintaining a consistent sleep schedule creating a relaxing bedtime routine and optimizing your sleep environment. In order to fall asleep at the same time and wake up refreshed you have to go to bed every day. A bedtime routine that includes activities such as reading A book taking A warm bath or practicing relaxation techniques can signal your body that it's time to relax and prepare for rest. A comfortable and quiet sleep environment with minimal distractions and a cool temperature can also improve the quality of sleep. By incorporating these basic sleep hygiene essentials into your daily routine you can maximize your sleep quality and increase your overall well-being.

DEFINITION AND IMPORTANCE OF SLEEP HYGIENE

Sleep hygiene refers to the practices and habits conducive to good Sleep on a regular basis. This includes maintaining a consistent sleep schedule creating a relaxing bedtime routine and ensuring that the sleep environment is comfortable and conducive to rest. Good sleep hygiene is crucial to overall health and well-being as sleep plays a vital role in mental function mood regulation and physical health. Poor sleep hygiene can lead to difficulties with concentration memory and decision-making as well as increase the risk of chronic health conditions such as diabetes obesity and cardiovascular disease. Having a proper sleep schedule is essential for improving the quality of life as individuals can improve their overall quality of life.

KEY COMPONENTS OF SLEEP HYGIENE

In some cases the sleep schedule should consist of a consistent schedule a relaxed bedtime and the optimal sleeping environment. By going to bed at the same time every day individuals can regulate their body's internal clock and improve their sleep quality. Engaging in calming activities such as reading a book or taking a warm bath before bed can help signal the body it's time to rest. Determining whether the bedroom is cool dark and quiet can create an ideal sleeping environment. Through incorporating these key components of sleep hygiene into their daily routine individuals can increase the likelihood of getting a sleepy night and ultimately improve their overall health and.

COMMON MISCONCEPTIONS ABOUT SLEEP HYGIENE

In spite of the growing body of research supporting the importance of sleeping hygiene in maintaining optimal health there are still a number of common misconceptions around this topic. Some misconceptions that exist are the belief that individuals can make up for lost sleep on the weekends. However studies show that attempting to sleep in this manner disrupts the body's natural sleep-wake cycle and can actually lead to a number of adverse health outcomes including an increase risk of obesity diabetes and cardiovascular. Another common misconception is that alcohol can be beneficial for sleep. While it's true that alcohol can make individuals feel drowsy in the initial stages but does actually disrupt the normal sleep cycle and overall leads to poor quality sleep. These misconceptions highlight the need for greater awareness around the importance of adopting healthy sleep habits to optimize one's overall health.

OPTIMIZING THE SLEEP ENVIRONMENT

The quality of sleep is essential for improving. It is important To consider factors such as lighting noise temperature and comfort in the bedroom To achieve this. One of the most important aspects in optimizing sleep environment is making it dark and quiet. Light and noise can disrupt the body's natural sleep-wake cycle making it difficult to fall asleep and stay asleep all night. The maintenance of a comfortable temperature in the bedroom is also important for promoting deep and restorative sleep. Making small adjustments to these factors in the sleep environment can have a significant impact on the overall quality of our rest and help us wake up each morning refreshed and rejuvenated.

IMPORTANCE OF A CONDUCIVE SLEEP SETTING

For optimal sleep quality and quantity the establishment of a conducive sleeping environment is crucial. The comfort of A relaxing environment can dramatically impact an individual's ability to fall asleep and stay asleep throughout the night. Factors like lighting temperature noise levels and comfort of the mattress and bed play a role in determining the overall sleep environment. By addressing these aspects and creating a place that encourages relaxation and comfort individuals can greatly improve their sleep hygiene and overall well-being. For enhancing sleep quality promoting restorative rest and ultimately improving cognitive functioning mood regulation and overall health it is imperative that a conducive sleep environment is prioritized.

ELEMENTS OF A COMFORTABLE SLEEP ENVIRONMENT

To obtain optimal health and quality of rest creating a comfortable sleep environment is essential. The use of top quality mattresses and pillows that provide optimal support and comfort is One of the key elements of a comfortable sleep environment. Keep a cool room temperature ideally between 60-67 degrees Fahrenheit can also help promote restful sleep. It is also important to reduce noise and light disturbances in the sleep environment as these factors can disrupt sleep patterns. The use of relaxing scents such as lavender or chamomile also helps the body tell when it's time to rest and relax. This can improve the quality of sleep and overall well-being By incorporating these elements into our sleep environment.

THE ROLE OF LIGHT AND NOISE CONTROL

Controlling light and noise levels plays a vital role In improving sleep quality In addition to maintaining a regular sleep schedule and creating a comfortable sleep environment. Exposure to bright light especially during the hours leading up to bedtime can disrupt the body's natural circadian rhythms and make it difficult to fall asleep. In addition excessive noise stimulation can inhibit the brain's transition into a restful state. By using blackout curtains to block out external light sources and investing in white noise machines to drown out disruptive sounds individuals can create a more conducive sleep environment that promotes deep rest. In addition setting a relaxing bedtime routine that minimizes exposure to both light and noise can signal the body that it is time to relax and prepare for sleep leading to more restful and rejuvenating nights.

BEDTIME RITUALS

Night rituals are essential for improving sleep quality and overall well-being. These rituals can help signal to the body and mind that it is time to rest. Some common bedtime rituals include reading a book listening to soothing music practicing relaxation techniques such as deep breathing or meditation or engaging in skincare routine. Setting a consistent bedtime routine can help regulate the body's internal clock and improve sleep quality. We can create a peaceful and relaxing environment that promotes a restful night's sleep By incorporating these rituals into our nightly routine. Bedtime rituals can additionally have a positive impact on our mental health by reducing stress and improving relaxation before bedtime.

ESTABLISHING A CONSISTENT BEDTIME ROUTINE

In terms of sleep quality and overall wellbeing this is critical. By going to bed every night at the same time and engaging in calming activities before bed such as reading or meditation individuals can signal to their bodies that it is time to rest and prepare for sleep. This routine helps regulate the body's internal clock making it easier for you to fall asleep and wake up at the same time each day. A consistent bedtime routine can also reduce the likelihood of sleep disorders like insomnia and other sleep disorders by promoting relaxation and reducing stress levels. Overall consistency in the bedtime routine is an important step to improve sleep and to maintain optimal health.

RELAXATION TECHNIQUES BEFORE BED

Before you fall asleep it is important to engage in relaxation techniques to help calm the mind and body for a good night's sleep. One effective technique is progressive muscle relaxation where One tenses and then releases each muscle group in the body gradually. It helps release physical tension and promotes a feeling of relaxation. Deep breathing exercises such as diaphragmatic breathing can also be helpful to reducing stress and preparing the body for sleep. In addition meditation or mindfulness practice can help focus the mind and bring awareness to the present moment allowing anxiety and worries to fade away. By incorporating these techniques into a routine at bedtime individuals can create a calm environment that promotes good sleep.

THE IMPACT OF PRE-SLEEP ACTIVITIES ON SLEEP QUALITY

Prior research suggests that sleep activities before bed have a significant impact on sleep quality. Engaging in calming activities such as reading a book practicing meditation or taking a warm bath before bed has been found to promote relaxation and possibly improve sleep outcomes. Conversely engaging in stimulating activities such as watching tv or using electronic devices can lead to decreased sleep quality and increased arousal. By integrating relaxation pre-sleep rituals into their nightly routines individuals may be able to improve the quality and duration of their sleep ultimately leading to improved overall well-being and cognitive functioning.

DIET

Diet and sleep are closely connected and eating what we eat can significantly affect the quality of sleep. Consuming sugary foods close to bedtime can disrupt our natural sleep cycles and lead to difficulty falling asleep during the night. On the other hand foods rich in tryptophan magnesium and melatonin such as turkey nuts and cherries can promote relaxation and help us relax into a restful sleep. Maintaining a consistent meal schedule and avoiding heavy meals right before bed can also help improve sleep hygiene. By paying attention to our diet and making mindful choices we can improve our overall sleep quality and wake up every day feeling refreshed and rejuvenated.

FOODS AND BEVERAGES THAT AFFECT SLEEP

Certain foods and beverages can negatively affect our sleep patterns. For example caffeine in coffee tea and chocolate is a stimulant which can disrupt sleep by increasing alertness and delaying the onset of sleep. It can cause drowsiness to feel at first but can also disrupt sleep later in the night by interrupting the sleep cycle. To increase the risk of indigestion heavy or spicy foods close to bedtime can make it difficult to fall asleep or stay asleep throughout the night. In order to promote better sleep quality it is important to be aware of what we consume before bedtime.

TIMING OF MEALS RELATIVE TO SLEEP

Another important factor to consider when trying to improve sleep is the time of meals relative to sleep. It is recommended to avoid heavy or large meals within a few hours of bedtime as this can cause pain and difficulty falling asleep. On the other hand going to bed hungry can also disturb sleep so it is important to find a balance and have a light snack if needed. Certain foods and beverages such as caffeine and alcohol can interfere with sleep and should be avoided in the hours leading up to bedtime. Overall taking care of the timing of meals can play a significant role in improving sleep quality.

NUTRITIONAL SUPPLEMENTS AND THEIR EFFECTS ON SLEEP

There is evidence that certain nutritional supplements can have a positive effect on sleep quality. Melatonin is a hormone that regulates sleep-wake cycles and can be taken as a supplement to promote relaxation and induce sleep. Magnesium is another important mineral that plays a role in regulating neurotransmitters involved in sleep. Studies have shown that magnesium can improve sleep quality and reduce sleepiness symptoms. Additionally certain herbs such as chamomile and valerian root have been used as natural sleep aids for centuries and can be found in supplement form. Although further research is needed to fully understand the effects of nutritional supplements on sleep incorporating these supplements into a balanced diet may offer a safe and effective way to improve sleep quality.

PHYSICAL ACTIVITY

Physical activity has a direct impact on the quality and duration of sleep. Studies have consistently shown that individuals who engage in physical activity experience more restful and deeper sleep compared to those who lead sedentary lifestyles. The National Sleep Foundation recommends a minimum of 150 minutes of moderate to vigorous physical activity per week to reap The sleep-promoting benefits of exercise. Not only does physical activity regulate the body's internal clock it also plays a crucial role in reducing symptoms of sleep apnea and insomnia. It is also clear that regular exercise can improve mood and overall well-being which can contribute to good sleep hygiene. In conclusion integrating regular physical activity into one's daily routine can be an effective strategy to improve sleep quality and overall health.

INFLUENCE OF EXERCISE ON SLEEP PATTERNS

Regular exercise has been shown to influence sleep patterns. Physical activity helps people fall asleep faster and achieve deeper more peaceful sleep. This is because exercise regulates the body's internal clock known as the circadian rhythm which controls when we feel awake and when we feel tired. Regular exercise can reduce the signs of insomnia and improve sleep quality. Studies have found that people who regularly exercise experience less incidents of waking up during the night and report feeling more refreshed and energized upon waking in the morning. It's very important to incorporate exercise into your daily routine it can even improve sleep health.

BEST TIMES FOR PHYSICAL ACTIVITY TO PROMOTE SLEEP

One of the best times to do physical activity to promote sleep is late afternoon or early evening. Exercising during this time can increase the body temperature which in turn can help trigger the release of melatonin which regulates sleep. Additionally engaging in physical activity during these times can help to reduce stress levels which can also help promote better sleep. Studies have shown that individuals who exercise regularly in the late afternoon or early evening experience a more restful sleep than those who do not engage in physical activity at different times of the day. So scheduling physical activity during these optimal times can play a significant role in improving sleep quality.

TYPES OF EXERCISE CONDUCIVE TO BETTER SLEEP

Regular exercise has been shown to improve sleep quality by helping to regulate the body's internal clock. Aerobic exercises such as running swimming and cycling have been found to be particularly helpful for sleep. These types of exercises help increase the amount of deep sleep people get leading to a more restorative sleep experience. Strength training and resistance training can also improve sleep by reducing symptoms of sleep apnea and insomnia. It is important for people to improve their sleep to incorporate a variety of exercises into their routine to reap maximum benefits.

STRESS MANAGEMENT FOR BETTER SLEEP

Is a stress-management technique effective in improving sleep quality?. Stress can affect our ability to relax and fall asleep leading to restless nights and poor sleep quality. The practice of mindful meditation breathing exercises and physical activity helps individuals to reduce stress and create a more conducive environment for restful sleep. Implementing these practices into a daily routine can not only help improve sleep but also contribute to overall mental and physical well-being. How do you manage stress effectively?.

RELATIONSHIP BETWEEN STRESS AND SLEEP

The relationship between sleep and stress is complex and bidirectional with each factor having an effect on The other in a cyclical manner. Psychological stress can affect the body's sleep patterns which can lead to difficulties falling asleep or staying asleep throughout the night. Lack of sleep In turn can create a vicious cycle that can be challenging to break. Research has shown that chronic stress activates the body's "fight or flight" response releasing hormones like cortisol that can interfere with the production of melatonin the hormone responsible for regulating sleep. Applying stress-reducing techniques such as mindfulness meditation or relaxation exercises can help improve sleep quality and break the cycle of stress and sleep disturbance.

STRESS REDUCTION TECHNIQUES FOR IMPROVED SLEEP

Techniques for Stress management play a crucial role in improving sleep quality. Chronic stress can disrupt the body's natural sleep cycle and cause difficulty falling asleep and staying asleep. By incorporating stress reduction techniques into one's daily routine individuals can effectively manage their stress levels and promote better sleep. Among the common strategies include meditation deep breathing exercises and progressive muscle relaxation. These techniques help to calm the mind and body reduce tension and promote a sense of relaxation making it easier to fall asleep and stay asleep during the night. By incorporating stress reduction techniques into daily routine individuals can successfully improve their overall sleep quality and achieve a more restful night's sleep.

THE ROLE OF STRESS MANAGEMENT IN SLEEP HYGIENE

Stress plays a key role in sleep hygiene. Chronic stress can significantly affect how much sleep a person 'gets every night'. The body's stress response system which is activated when individuals experience stressful situations can inhibit The ability to fall asleep and stay asleep. Meditation or mindfulness practices can help calm the mind and body before bedtime and promote better sleep. Through effective managing stress individuals can create a more conducive environment for restful and restorative sleep ultimately leading to better overall health and well-being.

COGNITIVE-BEHAVIORAL THERAPY FOR INSOMNIA

One widely studied and highly effective treatment for chronic Insomnia is Cognitive-Behavioral Therapy (CBT-I). CBT-I is a structured evidence-based approach which focuses on identifying and changing maladaptive thoughts and behaviors that contribute to poor sleep. This therapy generally involves several components including sleep limitation stimulative control cognitive therapy and relaxation techniques. CBT-I helps individuals develop healthier sleep habits and improve their overall sleep quality By addressing both cognitive and behavioral factors that perpetuate insomnia. Research has consistently shown that CBT-I is more effective over the long term than pharmacology alone and produces lasting improvements in sleep patterns and quality of life for individuals with chronic insomnia.

EXPLANATION OF CBT-I AND ITS EFFECTIVENESS

CBT-I is a highly effective treatment for people struggling with chronic sleep issues. This structured program typically contains components such as cognitive restructuring and stimulus control techniques sleep restriction therapy. CBT-I helps individuals develop healthier sleep patterns and improve sleep quality over time By targeting the underlying thoughts and behaviors that contribute to insomnia. Research consistently shows that CBT-I is more effective over a longer period compared to medication alone with lasting improvements in sleep duration and quality. CBT-I has also been found to have long lasting benefits that encompass not only improving sleep but also reduces anxiety and depression symptoms. CBT-I is a valuable and evidence-based approach to addressing insomnia and promoting better overall well-being.

CORE COMPONENTS OF CBT-I

Cognitive restructuring is one of the key components of CBT-I. This involves identifying and challenging negative thoughts and beliefs about sleep that may contribute to insomnia. By reframing these thoughts and replacing them with more positive and realistic beliefs people can reduce anxiety and stress around sleep making it easier to fall asleep and stay asleep. Another key component of CBT-I is sleep restriction which aims to consolidate sleep by limiting the time spent in bed to only when the individual actually sleeps. This helps to increase sleep efficiency and strengthen the association between sleeping and being in bed therefore improving overall sleep quality and duration. CBT-I core components may lead to significant improvements in sleep patterns and overall well-being for individuals suffering from insomnia.

HOW TO ACCESS CBT-I RESOURCES

Accessing clinical information for CBT-I can be a crucial step in improving sleep quality. There are several ways to get these resources. First individuals can find licensed therapists or sleep specialists trained in CBT-I techniques. They can provide personalized sessions to address specific sleep issues and develop a treatment plan that is customized for individual needs. There are also online resources and self-help guides available that can provide valuable information and techniques for the implementation of CBT-I strategies. These resources may include interactive programs sleep diary and relaxation exercises that can be accessed at any time. Access to CBT-I resources can help individuals develop healthier sleep habits and improve sleep quality.

MINDFULNESS AND MEDITATION

Another useful technique for improving sleep is meditation and mindfulness. Mindfulness involves being fully present in the moment which helps reduce racing thoughts and anxiety that often disrupt sleep. On the other hand meditation focuses on deep breathing and relaxation techniques to calm the mind and body. When incorporated into a nightly routine individuals can create a sense of peace and relaxation that can promote better sleep quality and duration. Studies show that regular meditation and mindfulness can lead to better sleep patterns and overall well-being. Hence incorporating these techniques into a daily bedtime routine can be a valuable tool for those looking to improve their sleep.

MINDFULNESS PRACTICES TO ENHANCE SLEEP

Mindfulness based meditation has been shown to improve sleep quality and promote relaxation before bedtime. By using mindfulness techniques such as deep breathing exercises body scans and meditation people can quiet their minds and decrease stress and anxiety levels that interfere with falling asleep. Research has shown that individuals who engage in regular mindfulness practices experience improved sleep patterns including a reduced time to fall asleep and an increase in total sleep duration. By incorporating mindfulness practices into their nightly routine individuals can create a relaxing environment which promotes restful sleep and overall well-being.

DIFFERENT MEDITATION TECHNIQUES FOR RELAXATION

For individuals seeking relaxation and improved sleep quality There are numerous meditation techniques available. One common technique is guided imagery meditation where individuals visualize soothing and peaceful scenes to promote relaxation. Another popular technique is mindful breathing meditation which focuses on breathing deeply and being present in the moment. Progressive muscle relaxation is another effective technique which involves the tightening and releasing muscle groups to reduce tension and promote relaxation. The love kindness meditation focuses on enhancing feelings of love and positive energy to self and others promoting feelings of compassion and reducing stress. By exploring and practicing different meditation techniques people can find the best method for relaxation and improving sleep quality.

STUDIES ON THE EFFECTIVENESS OF MINDFULNESS AND MEDITATION

Recent studies have shown that mindfulness and meditation practice improve sleep quality. For example a study by Black et al. (2020) found that participants who engaged in mindfulness meditation before bedtime experienced significant improvements in sleep latency and sleep efficiency compared to those who did not. A meta-analysis by Zhang et al. In studies (2019) demonstrated that mindfulness-based interventions are associated with decreased sleep anxiety symptoms and improved overall sleep quality. In addition this study suggests incorporating mindfulness and meditation into one's daily routine could be an important strategy for promoting better sleep health. Further research is needed to fully understand the mechanisms underlying these effects and explore the potential benefits of mindfulness and meditation for individuals with sleep disorders.

SLEEP SCHEDULING

Is a crucial aspect for a better quality of sleep. A consistent sleep schedule can help individuals regulate their internal body clock known as the circadian rhythm which plays a key role in determining the timing of sleep and wakefulness. This means going to bed every day and waking up at the same time even weekends to better synchronize the body's natural sleep-wake cycle. Disruptions to this schedule such as irregular bedtime or wake-up hours can cause sleep disturbances and contribute to issues such as insomnia. A consistent sleep schedule can also improve sleep efficiency and overall sleep quality promoting better cognitive functioning mood regulation and overall health.

THE CONCEPT OF SLEEP-WAKE SCHEDULING

One of the key concepts in sleep improvement techniques is the concept of sleep-wake scheduling. It involves establishing a consistent nighttime and wake-up time to regulate the body's internal clock known as the circadian rhythm. By going to bed at the same time each day people can train their bodies to fall asleep and wake up more easily leading to better sleep quality. The consistent sleep-wake schedule helps the body to get the necessary amount of rest each night which is essential for optimal functions during the day. In addition to setting a routine sleep wake schedule other techniques such as creating a relaxing bedtime routine and creating a comfortable sleep environment can further improve one's sleep quality.

STRATEGIES FOR FIXING A DISRUPTED SLEEP SCHEDULE

It is possible to set up a planned sleeping schedule with a sleep disorder by following several strategies. In order to regulate the internal clock of the body it must First and foremost establish a consistent bedtime and wake up time. This means going to bed and going to bed every day at the same time even on weekends. Second creating a bedtime routine that helps to signal the body that it is time to relax and prepare for sleep can be extremely helpful. This may include reading a book taking a warm bath or practicing relaxation techniques such as deep breathing or meditation. Avoiding caffeine and electronic devices near bedtime can also help promote better sleep. Providing a comfortable sleep environment that is dark quiet and cool can help you to restful sleep. By integrating these techniques into your daily routine you can effectively fix a disrupted sleep schedule and improve your overall sleep quality.

BENEFITS OF MAINTAINING A CONSISTENT SLEEP-WAKE CYCLE

Maintaining a consistent sleep-wake cycle has many beneficial effects that positively affect one's overall health and well-being. The cognitive function is improved and mental clarity is improved. If we go to bed regularly and wake up at the same times every day our bodies become accustomed to this routine which allows us to achieve a deeper and more restorative sleep. This in turn can result in a more focused memory retention and a more proficient decision making skills. A constant sleep-wake cycle may also help regulate our moods and emotions reducing the risk of experiencing mood swings and irritability. The study found that a regular sleep schedule also has been associated with a stronger immune system and a reduced risk of developing chronic health conditions such as diabetes and cardiovascular disease. Getting a consistent sleep cycle can lead to energy better mental acuity and better overall health.

THE ROLE OF TECHNOLOGY IN SLEEP IMPROVEMENT

Modern sleep improvement techniques use Technology as a critical role. From intelligent beds that adjust to individual sleep patterns to sleep tracking apps that monitor the quality of sleep technology has revolutionized the way we understand and improve our sleep. For example Fitbit and Apple Watch can track sleep patterns and provide valuable insights into sleep cycles and durations. Sleep noise machines and white noise apps can create a relaxing environment conducive to better sleep. Technology has also allowed the development of sleep coaching apps and online programs that provide personal recommendations for improving sleep quality. Technology has become an essential tool in the quest for better sleep and overall well-being.

SLEEP TRACKING DEVICES AND THEIR USES

Recent years have seen the use of sleeping tracking devices increasing as more people prioritize their overall health and wellness. These devices use sensors and accelerometers to monitor various aspects of sleep including duration quality and patterns. By providing users with detailed information on their sleep habits these devices can help individuals identify areas for improvement and make necessary adjustments to their bedtime routine. Several devices even offer personalized recommendations for better sleep such as controlling room temperature or incorporating relaxation techniques. Sleep tracking devices provide valuable tools for improving sleep quality and improving general well-being.

APPS FOR SLEEP ENHANCEMENT

One of the promising advances in the field of sleep improvement techniques is the development of apps specifically designed to improve sleep quality. These apps utilize a variety of techniques such as guided meditation white noise and sleep tracking features to help users achieve a more restful night's sleep. Some apps even use data from wearable devices such as fitness trackers to provide personalized recommendations for improving sleep habits. These apps have the potential to reach a wide audience and have a significant impact on the quality of sleep for many individuals With the increasing prevalence of smartphones and wearable technology. While further research is needed to fully understand the efficacy of these apps preliminary studies have shown promising results in terms of improving sleep quality and overall health.

LIMITING EXPOSURE TO BLUE LIGHT BEFORE BEDTIME

Is essential for better sleep. Blue light produced by electronic devices including smartphones tablets and computers can interfere with the body's production of melatonin the hormone which regulates sleep-wake cycles. Research has shown that blue light exposure before bedtime can disrupt the natural sleep patterns and lead to difficulty falling asleep. To reduce this effect it is recommended To limit screen time at least an hour before bedtime and use blue light filters or glasses To minimize exposure. Using these strategies individuals can promote a healthier sleep environment and improve overall sleep quality.

PHARMACOLOGICAL AIDS FOR SLEEP

One of the most widely used pharmacological aids for sleep is melatonin a hormone that regulates the sleep-wake cycle. Melatonin supplement is commonly used to treat insomnia and jet lag as well as to improve sleep quality. Another commonly prescribed sleep medication is benzodiazepines which enhance the effects of the neurotransmitter GABA in the brain to induce relaxation and sleep. These medications however can be habit-forming and may have side effects such as drowsiness and decreased coordination. Before using pharmacological support for sleep It is important to consult a healthcare provider to ensure they are safe and appropriate for individual needs.

OVERVIEW OF PRESCRIPTION SLEEP MEDICATIONS

Many people who are experiencing trouble sleeping or other sleep related difficulties turn to prescription sleep medications for help. These drugs work by targeting different receptors in the brain to induce drowsiness or inhibit wakefulness. Some common prescription sleep medications are benzodiazepines sedatives hypnotics non-benzodiazepine and melatonin receptor agonists. While these drugs can be effective in improving sleep they also come with potentially dangerous side effects and risks such as dependence tolerance and drowsiness the next day. When you are considering sleeping medication It is important for individuals to discuss the potential benefits and risks with a healthcare provider before starting treatment.

RISKS AND BENEFITS OF SLEEP-INDUCING DRUGS

Sleep-inducing drugs can be a useful tool for individuals suffering from insomnia or other sleep disorders as they provide quick relief and allow for a more restful night's sleep. These drugs however come with potential risks and side effects that should be carefully considered. One major risk of sleep induced drugs is the potential for dependence and addiction as individuals may become dependent on the medication to fall asleep. Many drugs can also cause drowsiness and impair cognitive function the next day leading to decreased productivity and possible safety concerns. It is important for individuals to weigh the benefits of sleep against these risks and to work closely with a healthcare provider to find the best treatment plan for their individual needs.

HERBAL AND NATURAL SLEEP AIDS

Can be useful to improve the quality of sleep. Many people turn to options such as lavender essential oil valerian root melatonin chamomile tea and lavender for relaxation and sleep. These substances are often seen as gentler alternatives to prescription sleep medications sometimes associated with unwanted side effects or dependence. While research is still ongoing to determine the effectiveness of natural sleep aids many individuals report finding relief from their sleep issues with the help of these supplements. Before starting a sleep regimen It is important to consult a healthcare provider especially if you are currently taking other medications or have underlying health conditions.

NAPPING STRATEGIES

When it comes to napping strategies there are several important factors to consider in order to maximize the benefits of a short nap. One important aspect is to choose the right time of day to nap generally in the early afternoon when the body experiences a natural dip in energy levels. It is also essential to find a quiet and dark environment to nap in order to create a conducive environment for sleep. Another key strategy is to keep naps short ideally around 20-30 minutes to avoid entering deep stages of sleep that can leave one feeling groggy and disorient. The following guidelines help individuals incorporate napping into their daily routine to enhance alertness memory and cognitive performance.

BENEFITS AND DRAWBACKS OF NAPPING

One of the most controversial topics in recent sleep research is the benefit and drawbacks of napping. On one hand napping has been shown to have numerous positive effects On cognition mood and overall alertness. A short nap can help improve memory increase creativity and improve focus making it A useful tool for students and professionals alike. However napping can also have negative effects such as disrupting sleep patterns at night and causing grogginess on the night. Likewise some people find it difficult to fall asleep if they nap too late in the day. Strategic napping can be a powerful tool for maximizing productivity and improving overall wellbeing Despite these drawbacks.

GUIDELINES FOR EFFECTIVE NAPPING

One guideline for effective napping is to keep them short generally between 20 and 30 minutes in order to avoid entering deep
stages of sleep that can leave One feeling groggy upon awakening. It is also important to nap at the right time of day ideally
in the early afternoon when the body experiences a natural slug-
gish in energy levels. Create a comfortable and quiet environment conducive to relaxation can help maximize the benefits of
napping. As part of this relaxation techniques such as deep
breathing or meditation can help promote a faster and more
effective sleep. Lastly it is recommended to set an alarm to prevent oversleeping and disrupting sleep patterns. By following
these guidelines individuals can experience the rejuvenating effects of napping without negatively affecting their overall sleep
quality.

UNDERSTANDING THE TIMING AND DURATION OF NAPS

Is crucial to the optimal benefits of rest as it must not have negative effects on nighttime sleep. Research suggests that the ideal time to nap is early afternoon around 1 to 3 pm when the body's natural circadian rhythm tends to dip leading to a natural decrease in alertness. Naps taken later in the day can interfere with the ability to fall asleep at night while long napping can lead to grogginess upon awakening known as sleep inertia (greater than 30 minutes). Individuals seeking to incorporate naps into their daily routine should therefore aim for a short duration and strategic timing to reap the rejuvenating benefits of rest without disrupting nighttime sleep patterns.

AGING

As adults changes in sleep patterns are common. This is due to a variety of factors including changes in circadian rhythms decreased production of certain hormones and an increased prevalence of medical conditions which can disrupt sleep. Adults over 65 often experience a decline in slow wave sleep and an increase in sleep fragmentation leading to more frequent awakenings during the night. These changes may result in symptoms such as insomnia sleepiness and fatigue during the daytime. Fortunately there are several strategies that can help older adults improve sleep quality such as maintaining a consistent sleep schedule creating a relaxing bedtime routine and avoiding caffeine and alcohol near bedtime. By using these sleep improvement techniques older adults can potentially improve sleep quality and overall well-being in the aging process.

CHANGES IN SLEEP PATTERNS WITH AGE

As we age our sleep patterns undergo significant changes that can affect our overall quality of sleep. Research has shown that older adults experience a shift towards lighter sleep that is more easily disrupted leading to more frequent awakenings throughout the night. As with age the amount of time spent in deep restorative sleep decreases causing feelings of fatigue and decreasing cognitive function during the day. These changes in sleep patterns are often attributed to age-related hormonal shifts as well as health conditions which become more common as we get older. Implementing sleep improvement techniques such as establishing a consistent bedtime routine avoiding stimulants before bed and creating a comfortable sleep environment can help mitigate some of the effects of age-related changes in sleep patterns and promote better overall sleep quality.

SLEEP DISORDERS MORE COMMON IN OLDER ADULTS

Older adults are more susceptible to sleeping disorders due to a variety of factors compared to younger individuals. As we grow older our sleep patterns change resulting in lighter and more fragmented sleep. This can result in frequent awakenings at night and difficulty falling asleep. Older adults are also more likely to suffer from medical conditions such as sleep apnea restless leg syndrome and insomnia which can interfere with sleep. A number of other factors such as the decreased production of certain hormones in the body can also contribute to sleep disturbances in older adults. For older people It is important to address these issues and seek treatment in order to improve their quality of sleep and overall health.

TAILORING SLEEP IMPROVEMENT TECHNIQUES FOR SENIORS

Has to understand the inherent challenges that come with aging. As we get older our sleep patterns change with many seniors experiencing lighter and more fragmented sleep. For this to be addressed it is important to consider a variety of factors such as changes In circadian rhythms medication side effects and underlying health conditions. Similarly implementing strategies that promote relaxation and stress reduction such as mindfulness meditation or gentle stretching exercises can be beneficial for seniors struggling with sleep disturbances. Healthcare professionals can better support seniors in achieving restful and rejuvenating sleep By recognizing and addressing the specific needs of older adults.

DIFFERENT CULTURES

During the study of sleep In different cultures it becomes apparent that different societies have unique customs and beliefs about rest and rejuvenation. For example sleep is considered essential in traditional Chinese medicine For overall well-being and maintaining equilibrium in the body. It is used acupuncture and herbal remedies to treat sleep disorders and to promote restful sleep. The Maasai tribe In Kenya values sleep as a sign of weakness and pride themselves on their ability to function with minimal rest. This cultural attitude to sleep reflects deeply held beliefs about strength and resilience. We gain a greater understanding of how different societies prioritize rest and its impact on health and daily life.

CULTURAL ATTITUDES TOWARDS SLEEP

The differences between different peoples and different times are large. Sleep is often viewed as a necessary but secondary aspect of life In some cultures such as those In Western societies with productivity and achievement taking precedence over rest and relaxation. In contrast sleep is highly valued and seen In some Asian cultures as crucial for overall well-being and functioning. In these cultures napping during the day or getting a full night's rest is often prioritized and even encouraged. These differences in culture can have significant impacts on people's sleep habits and general health. Understanding and respecting these cultural differences can help individuals develop more effective sleep improvement techniques tailored to their specific cultural attitudes and beliefs.

SLEEP PRACTICES AROUND THE WORLD

The beliefs and traditions within the culture of the nation are vastly different. In some countries such as Japan it is common and even encouraged to take short naps during the day to improve productivity. In contrast In Western countries such as the United states it's generally recommended to have seven hours of sleep each night. In addition it is not uncommon for people to have a siesta in the afternoon in some Mediterranean countries to combat the midday slump. Understanding the different sleep practices around the world can provide valuable insight into how different cultures prioritize rest and relaxation. By incorporating these practices into our own routines we can improve our sleep quality and well-being.

HOW CULTURAL NORMS INFLUENCE SLEEP HYGIENE

Culture plays a significant role in shaping individuals' beliefs behaviors and practices around sleep hygiene. Cultural norms influence how people prioritize sleep manage their sleep schedules and the importance of rest. For example some cultures may value productivity and hard work over adequate rest leading people to sacrifice sleep to satisfy societal expectations. Other cultures may place a high emphasis on relaxation and self-care promoting healthy sleep habits as a means of maintaining overall well-being. Further cultural practices like bedtime rituals meal timing and technology use before sleep can influence individuals' sleep quality and duration. Understanding the influence of cultural norms on sleep hygiene individuals can assess their own beliefs and practices surrounding sleep and make informed decisions to prioritize rest and improve their overall health and well-being.

GENDER DIFFERENCES

Research has shown that between men and women there are significant differences in sleep patterns and behaviors. Men are more likely to develop sleep disorders such as sleep apnea while women are more likely to experience insomnia and restless leg syndrome. Also hormonal fluctuations throughout the menstrual cycle can impact the quality and quantity of sleep a woman needs. Women generally have a longer duration of slow wave sleep which is important for memory consolidation and overall cognitive function. Understanding these gender differences in sleep can lead to more effective and tailored sleep interventions for both men and women.

SLEEP DIFFERENCES BETWEEN MEN AND WOMEN

Research shows that there are significant differences in sleep patterns between men and women. Women experience more disrupted sleep throughout their menstrual cycle due to hormonal fluctuations. A higher prevalence of insomnia and restless leg syndrome compared to men. On the other hand men are more likely to suffer from sleep apnea and other breathing disorders which can significantly affect the quality of sleep. These differences in sleep patterns highlight the importance of taking into account gender-specific factors when developing strategies to improve sleep quality and overall well-being for both men and women.

HORMONAL INFLUENCES ON SLEEP

Hormones play a crucial role in regulating sleep patterns and overall sleep quality. One key hormone involved in sleep-wake cycle is melatonin which is produced in response to darkness by the pineal gland and helps the body signal that it's time to sleep. Cortisol also plays a role in regulating sleep by helping to keep individuals alert and awake during the day. But disruptions in hormone levels such as those caused by stress or hormonal imbalances can lead to poor sleep quality and difficulties falling asleep. Therefore it is important to maintain a balanced balance of hormones to support healthy sleep patterns and overall well-being.

GENDER-SPECIFIC SLEEP IMPROVEMENT STRATEGIES

The differences between the human body and the environment can impact on sleep patterns and quality of sleep. Women suffer from insomnia due to hormonal fluctuations while men suffer sleep apnea and snoring. Thus tailored strategies can be beneficial in addressing specific issues for each gender. For women using relaxation techniques and establishing a consistent sleep schedule can help regulate their sleep cycles. On the other hand men may benefit from weight management strategies and positional therapy to improve breathing during sleep. By recognizing these differences and implementing gender specific sleep improvement strategies individuals can optimize their sleep and overall wellbeing.

OCCUPATIONAL HEALTH

In the workplace the amount of sleep a person receives is One of the key factors that affect occupational health. Sleep deprivation can lead to a variety of negative consequences including impaired cognitive function decreased productivity and an increased risk of accidents and injuries at work. It is vital for individuals to prioritize their sleep health and implement strategies to improve the quantity and quality of their sleep. This may include setting a regular sleep schedule creating a comfortable sleep environment and practicing relaxation techniques before bed. Sleep habits can help individuals improve their overall performance and elicit greater work productivity.

IMPACT OF SHIFT WORK ON SLEEP

Shift work which involves working outside of typical daytime hours such as weekends or nights can have a significant impact on sleep patterns. Shift workers often experience disruptions in their natural circadian rhythm which can cause difficulty falling asleep and staying asleep. This can result in decreased sleep quality and quantity which can negatively affect cognitive function mood and overall well-being. The negative effects of shift work on sleep can be mitigated by maintaining a consistent sleep schedule creating a dark and quiet sleep environment and avoiding stimulants like caffeine close to bedtime. Working with the right lifestyle and good sleep hygiene workers can improve sleep quality and overall health.

STRATEGIES FOR SHIFT WORKERS TO IMPROVE SLEEP

For shift workers looking to improve sleep can be highly beneficial implementing strategic changes to their daily routine. One effective strategy is to establish a consistent sleep schedule even during the weekends to regulate the body's internal clock. Furthermore creating a dark quiet and cool sleeping environment can improve sleep quality. It is also important for shift workers to limit exposure before bed to screens and artificial light as these can disrupt the body's natural sleep-wake cycle. Finally relaxing techniques such as deep breathing exercises or meditation before bedtime can help calm the mind and prepare the body for sleep. Workers can improve their sleep quality By incorporating these strategies into their daily routine and promote better overall health and well-being.

OCCUPATIONAL HAZARDS RELATED TO POOR SLEEP

One of the occupational hazards associated with poor sleep is the increased risk of workplace injuries. When people are deprived of sleep their cognitive abilities reaction times and decision-making skills are impaired which puts them at higher risk for accidents or making mistakes at work. This can be particularly dangerous in high-risk professions such as medical construction or transport where even a small mistake can have serious consequences. Furthermore chronic sleep deprivation has been linked to a higher chance of developing chronic conditions such as heart disease and obesity which can also impact an individual's ability to perform their job effectively over time. The well-being of your employees and their health are essential for employers to promote healthy sleep habits to prevent these occupational hazards from occurring.

SLEEP AND ACADEMIC PERFORMANCE

The amount and quality of sleep a student receives is One of the most significant factors affecting academic performance. Recent research has found that poor sleep habits can negatively affect academic success. The researchers wrote that students who didn't get enough sleep were more likely to get poor grades and struggle with concentration In class. This is because sleep plays a crucial role in memory retention and cognitive function. To improve academic performance students should prioritize getting at least 7-9 hours of sleep every night and practice good sleep hygiene techniques such as maintaining a consistent sleep schedule creating a relaxing bedtime routine and avoiding electronic devices before bed. Investing in sleep can enhance students academic performance and overall success in classroom.

CORRELATION BETWEEN SLEEP AND LEARNING

Numerous studies have demonstrated a strong correlation between sleep and learning. Adequate sleep is important for cognitive function memory consolidation and information retention. When people do not get enough sleep their ability to focus problem solving and learn new information is severely impaired. Research has shown that while sleeping the brain processes and stores new information which is easier to remember and apply later. Sleep deprivation has been linked to reduced academic performance lower test scores and reduced overall productivity. So having adequate sleep hygiene and better quality of rest can greatly increase learning and academic success.

SLEEP STRATEGIES FOR STUDENTS

Creating a consistent sleep schedule is an important sleep strategy for students. Go to bed at the same time every day helps regulate your internal clock making it easier to fall asleep and wake up refreshed. Another useful strategy is to create a relaxing bedtime routine that signals your body to relax and prepare for sleep. This could include reading a book taking a warm bath or practicing relaxation techniques such as breathing deep and meditation. It is further important for students to create a sleep-induring environment by keeping their bedroom dark quiet and cool. Eliminating stimulants like caffeine and electronics before bed can improve sleep quality. By implementing these sleep strategies students can improve their academic performance and overall well-being.

ADDRESSING SLEEP ISSUES IN ACADEMIC SETTINGS

Is essential to the academic success of students and their overall well-being. Lack of sleep has been linked to lower cognitive function memory problems and difficulties learning and retaining information. This can greatly impact a student's learning in class and in the academic assessment. To address these issues universities may implement strategies such as promoting healthy sleep habits providing resources for stress management and offering support services for students experiencing chronic sleep problems. By prioritizing the importance of sleep and providing resources for students to improve their sleep quality academic institutions can help students reach their full potential and thrive in academic endeavors.

ATHLETIC PERFORMANCE

Sleep plays a crucial role in athletic performance as this is the time that the body recovers and repairs itself. Shorter or poor quality sleep can lead to reduced reaction times impaired cognitive function and decreased endurance. In fact research has shown that athletes who have 7-9 hours sleep per night are more prone to injury and lower overall performance. For improving sleep quality and duration athletes can implement various strategies such as creating a consistent sleep schedule setting a bedtime routine and creating a sleep-friendly environment. By promoting sleep athletes can optimize their performance and recovery leading to better results in their athletic endeavors.

THE IMPORTANCE OF SLEEP FOR ATHLETES

Sleep is essential For optimal performance and recovery. Sleep plays a crucial role in regulating hormones such as human growth hormone this hormone is essential for muscle repair and growth. A good sleep is also necessary for the proper functioning of the brain reaction time and decision making abilities all of which are crucial for athletic performance. Sleep deprivation can cause decreased endurance strength and coordination as well as an increased risk of injury. For optimal athletic potential athletes should prioritize getting 7-9 hours of sleep per night. The following tips will help athletes improve their sleep quality and overall performance on the field.

SLEEP OPTIMIZATION TECHNIQUES FOR SPORTS PERFORMANCE

Sleep optimization techniques are essential for athletes who want to improve their performance at the gym or on the field. Research has shown that getting enough sleep can enhance athletic abilities such as speed strength and reaction time. For optimal sleep athletes should aim to get 7-9 hours of sleep per night establish a consistent sleep schedule create a relaxing bedtime routine and optimize their sleep environment by keeping it dark silent and cool. Athletes can also benefit from avoiding stimulants like caffeine and electronic devices before bed as well as incorporating relaxation techniques such as deep breathing or meditation to promote restful sleep. Through the proper sleep practices and the proper management of the performance of athletes these optimization techniques can increase their athletic performance and reach their goals on the field.

CASE STUDIES OF SLEEP INTERVENTIONS IN ATHLETICS

One example of a successful case study of sleep intervention in athletics is that of the men's basketball team of Stanford university. The team participated in a sleep education program that aimed at improving their sleep habits and ultimately improving their athletic performance. The program included providing information about The importance of sleep for recovery and performance as well as providing strategies for improving sleep quality such as setting consistent bedtimes creating a calm bedtime routine and limiting exposure to screens before bed. The players reported feeling more rested and alert during games and practices which led to an increase in their overall performance on the court. This case study highlights the potential impact of sleep interventions on athletic performance and highlights the importance of prioritizing sleep in sports training programs.

MENTAL HEALTH

Sleep plays a vital role in maintaining optimal mental health as during deep Sleep the brain is able to process emotions and consolidate memories. However many individuals struggle with sleep disturbances such as sleep apnea or insomnia which can have negative effects on their mental well-being. Research has actually shown that sleep deprivation is associated with an increased risk of psychiatric disorders such as depression and anxiety. Therefore it is crucial to maintain mental health for a good night's sleep and seek treatment for sleep disorders. By implementing simple sleep routines such as breathing relaxation techniques before bed and avoiding stimulants like caffeine and electronics at night individuals can improve the quality of sleep and in turn support their mental health.

CONNECTION BETWEEN SLEEP AND PSYCHOLOGICAL WELL-BEING

The relationship between sleep and psychological well-being is complex and multifaceted. Research has consistently shown that sleep can have a detrimental effect on one's mental health. Sleep deprivation has been linked to elevated levels of depression anxiety and stress. Sleep plays a crucial role in memory development and emotional regulation. On the other hand adequate and restful sleep has been associated with enhanced mood cognition and overall well-being. Keeping a consistent sleep schedule creating a relaxing bedtime routine and creating a comfortable sleeping environment can help improve both the quantity and the quality of sleep thereby enhancing psychological well-being.

SLEEP DISTURBANCES ASSOCIATED WITH MENTAL HEALTH CONDITIONS

Sleep disturbances are commonly associated with mental health problems like schizophrenia bipolar disorder and anxiety depression. Research has shown that those with these conditions often have difficulties falling asleep sustaining a steady sleep schedule and maintaining a constant sleep. These disturbances can exacerbate symptoms of the underlying mental health condition resulting in a vicious cycle of sleep deprivation and worsened mental. It is important for people with mental health conditions to address their sleep disturbances in order to improve overall wellbeing and quality of life. Various techniques such as CBT-I and relaxation techniques have been shown to be effective in improving sleep for individuals with mental health conditions.

APPROACHES TO IMPROVE SLEEP IN THE CONTEXT OF MENTAL HEALTH

Involve a multifaceted approach that addresses both psychological and biological factors. CBT-I is shown to be an effective treatment for sleep disturbances in individuals with mental health disorders. This therapy focuses on addressing cognitive distortions and maladaptive behaviors which contribute to poor sleep quality. In addition CBT-I mindfulness-based interventions such as meditation and yoga have been found to be beneficial for improving sleep In those with mental health problems. These practices help individuals increase awareness of their thoughts emotions and body sensations which promote relaxation and reduce anxiety and stress levels that interfere with sleep. Incorporating lifestyle changes such as regular exercise a balanced diet and a consistent sleep schedule can further improve sleep quality and overall mental well-being. By adopting a comprehensive approach that addresses both the mental and physical aspects of sleep individuals can experience significant improvements in their sleep patterns and quality of life.

CHRONIC ILLNESS

Chronic diseases can affect sleep quality and quantity leading to a vicious cycle of worsening symptoms and decreased ability to deal with daily life. Conditions such as fibromyalgia multiple sclerosis and chronic pain syndromes disrupt the sleep cycle leading to fatigue irritability and cognitive impairment. In order to manage these symptoms effectively and improve overall quality of life people with chronic illnesses must prioritize their sleep health. Adopting relaxation techniques creating a consistent sleep schedule and seeking medical treatment for sleep disturbances are all crucial steps in the direction of achieving better sleep and managing the symptoms of chronic illnesses. By addressing the intersection of sleep and chronic illness individuals can improve their overall health and well-being.

IMPACT OF CHRONIC DISEASES ON SLEEP

Chronic diseases can significantly impact the quality of sleep of an individual. Diabetes heart disease and arthritis have been linked to various sleep disturbances including insomnia sleep apnea and restless leg syndrome. These disturbances in sleep patterns can further exacerbate the symptoms and the progression of These chronic diseases creating a vicious cycle of poor health outcomes. In addition lack of sleep can affect the immune system making individuals more likely to develop other chronic illnesses. Furthermore the effect of chronic diseases on sleep is essential for overall health and well-being. The introduction of lifestyle modifications such as regular exercise stress management techniques and proper sleep hygiene practices can improve sleep quality and mitigate the negative effects of chronic diseases on sleep.

MANAGING SLEEP WITH CHRONIC HEALTH CONDITIONS

For many individuals it can be difficult to do. Conditions such as diabetes arthritis and fibromyalgia affect the quality of sleep a person gets each night. To manage sleep well with these conditions it is important To establish a consistent bedtime routine prioritize relaxation techniques such as meditation or deep breathing exercises and create a comfortable sleep environment conducive To sleep. Working with a healthcare provider to address any underlying health issues that may be contributing to sleep disturbances is likewise essential to improving overall sleep quality. A person with chronic health conditions can take steps towards better managing their sleep and improving their overall wellbeing By implementing these strategies.

SLEEP AS A COMPONENT OF CHRONIC DISEASE MANAGEMENT

Sleep plays a crucial role In chronic disease management In the overall health and wellbeing. Research has shown that poor sleep can exacerbate the symptoms of chronic diseases such as diabetes cardiovascular disease and obesity. Therefore incorporating sleep-aware techniques into treatment plans can be an effective strategy to manage chronic conditions. By dealing with sleep disorders healthcare providers can help patients improve their physiological processes improve immune function and enhance cognitive function. In addition optimizing sleep can help improve adherence to treatment regimens and improve overall quality of life for individuals living with chronic diseases. So recognizing the importance of sleep in chronic disease management and implementing evidence-based strategies can significantly influence patient outcomes and overall health.

PAIN MANAGEMENT

Sleep plays a crucial role in chronic pain management. Research has shown that those who suffer from chronic pain experience disruptions in their sleep patterns leading to a vicious cycle of increased pain and poor sleep quality. Lack of sleep can lower pain thresholds and make pain feel more intense while pain can interfere with the ability to fall asleep and stay asleep. It is important for people with chronic pain to prioritize good sleep hygiene practices and to seek treatment options such as cognitive-behavioral therapy to improve their sleep quality. Using the proper treatment of sleep disturbances individuals can possibly reduce their perception of pain and improve their overall quality of life.

RELATIONSHIP BETWEEN SLEEP AND PAIN PERCEPTION

Studies show a clear correlation between sleep and pain perception lack of quality sleep is associated with heightened pain sensitivity. Sleep deprivation can increase the release of inflammatory markers in the body which in turn can exacerbate pain conditions. Poor sleep can further affect the brain's ability to regulate pain signals leading to a lower tolerance for pain. Conversely improving sleep quality through strategies such as creating a regular sleep schedule a relaxing bedtime routine and practicing relaxation techniques can help alleviate pain symptoms and improve overall well-being. This highlights the importance of maintaining good sleep habits as the best way to manage pain perception and overall health.

SLEEP IMPROVEMENT AS A PAIN MANAGEMENT STRATEGY

One promising pain management strategy is to improve sleep quality. Research has shown that those who have chronic pain have disturbed sleep patterns which can exacerbate their pain symptoms. Creating a relaxing bedtime routine and optimizing the sleep environment individuals with chronic pain may be able to experience a reduction in their pain levels By focusing on improving sleep hygiene habits such as maintaining a consistent sleep schedule. Additionally practicing relaxation techniques such as deep breathing or progressive muscle relaxation before bed can help quiet the mind and promote a more restful night's sleep. In addition treating sleep disturbances as part of a comprehensive pain management plan may lead to significant improvements in both sleep quality and pain levels for individuals with chronic pain conditions.

TECHNIQUES TO ALLEVIATE PAIN FOR BETTER SLEEP

One effective technique to relieve pain for better sleep is through relaxation techniques. By practicing techniques such as deep breathing progressive muscle relaxation and guided imagery individuals can reduce muscle tension reduce stress levels and promote a sense of calm before bed. These relaxation techniques help to distract the mind from pain this allows for better sleep quality. Additionally engaging in gentle yoga poses or stretches can help to release tight muscles and improve circulation aiding in pain relief. Other helpful practices include ensuring a good sleep hygiene like creating a comfortable sleep environment establishing a consistent bedtime routine and limiting screen time before bed. These techniques can be added into a daily routine to help alleviate pain and promote better sleep.

PARENTHOOD

Sleep becomes a luxury In the complex and demanding role of parenthood that is often sacrificed In order to address children's needs. When a baby arrives sleepless nights are inevitable as parents adjust to the demands of round-the-clock care and soothing. As children age parents may continue to face sleep disturbances whether it be from nightmares sickness or simply the normal challenges of raising a family. Depending on the extent of sleep deprivation it is a daily or weekly practice that can take a toll on a parent's physical and mental health which makes it crucial for them to prioritize their own sleep health in order to effectively care for their. A consistent bedtime routine and a conducive sleep environment can help parents navigate the challenges of sleep and parenthood.

SLEEP CHALLENGES FOR NEW PARENTS

One of the biggest challenges facing new parents is the lack of sleep that comes with caring for a newborn baby. The constant waking up at night to take care of The baby's needs can leave parents feeling overwhelmed and exhausted. In addition to the physical toll that sleep deprivation can take on new parents it can also negatively affect their emotional well-being and ability to function during the. The need for improving sleep quality for parents and baby is fundamental to ensure everyone has the rest they need to remain healthy and happy.

STRATEGIES FOR IMPROVING SLEEP WITH AN INFANT

For many new parents the challenge of sleeping with A baby can be overwhelming. While babies require a lot of attention it is important to prioritize and find effective strategies for improving sleep both for the infant and parents. One strategy is establishing a consistent bedtime routine that signals to the baby that it's time to rest and prepare for sleep. This can include activities such as bathing reading a story and gentle rocking or singing. Another important strategy is to create a conducive sleep environment with a comfortable temperature minimal noise and light and a safe sleep area for the infant. The addition of relaxing techniques such as swaddling white noise machines or pacifiers can help infants relax and settle into sleep more easily. Parents can work together to ensure a more relaxing and peaceful sleep experience for both themselves and their child By incorporating these strategies into their routine.

BALANCING CHILDCARE AND SLEEP NEEDS

Can be a difficult task for parents especially when it involves balancing many responsibilities such as school or work. Lack of sleep can have negative effects on both physical and mental health as well as their ability to effectively care for their children. To address this issue it is important for parents To establish a consistent bedtime routine for both their children and themselves. This can include setting a designated time for bed creating a calm and comfortable sleep environment and avoiding stimulating activities before bedtime. Parents may need to prioritize their self-care and seek support from family members or professional childcare services to ensure they are getting adequate rest while also meeting the needs of their children. Parents can enhance their overall well-being By effectively managing their sleep and childcare responsibilities and strengthen their ability to care for their children effectively.

TRAVEL

Sleep and travel are important components of overall well-being but can often conflict with one another. Travel whether it is for work or for leisure can disrupt our natural sleep patterns due to factors such as jet lag unfamiliar surroundings and irregular schedules. Generally using sleep improvement techniques to reduce sleep issues can help mitigate these challenges and ensure that we continue to prioritize rest even while on the go. Strategies such as maintaining a consistent sleep schedule create a soothing bedtime routine and make the sleep environment as comfortable as possible can all help in improving sleep quality during travel. By recognizing the importance of sleep and implementing these techniques we can better navigate the demands of travel while still allowing ourselves to prioritize our overall health and wellness.

MANAGING SLEEP DURING TRAVEL

One important aspect of ensuring sleep during travel is maintaining a consistent sleep schedule. It can be difficult to adapt to new sleep routines When traveling in different time zones. To help reduce jet lag and ensure a good night's sleep it is important To try To stick as much To your normal bedtime and wake-up time as possible. Other helpful tips include eliminating caffeine and alcohol before bed creating a relaxing bedtime routine and making sure your sleeping environment is comfortable and conducive to rest. The importance of sleep is enhanced during vacation By putting these strategies into place.

COPING WITH JET LAG

One common problem with long distance travel is dealing with jet lag. Jetlag occurs when our internal clock or circadian rhythm is disrupted by traveling across time zones. Jet lag Symptoms include tiredness concentrating difficulties irritability and disrupted sleep patterns. The symptoms of jet lag can be relieved through several different strategies. These include gradually adjusting sleep schedules before leaving exposure to natural light upon arrival to help reset the body clock staying hydrated and avoiding caffeine and alcohol. Furthermore a good diet can also help you reduce jet lag. Creating coping mechanisms can reduce the impact of jet lag and enjoy a more relaxing and rejuvenating trip.

TIPS FOR SLEEPING WELL ON THE ROAD

One of the challenges of traveling frequently is the importance of maintaining a good night's sleep while on the road. To ensure better quality and quantity of sleep it is important To establish a consistent bedtime routine even when away from home. This routine can include activities such as reading a book listening to soothing music or taking a bath before bed. Likewise it is rec-ommended to bring familiar items such as a favorite pillow or blanket to create a sense of comfort and familiarity in a new environment. Another tip to sleep well on the road is to choose accommodations that offer soundproofing and offer comfortable mattresses and bedding. In order to reduce cravings of caffeine and alcohol it is also important to avoid heavy meals close to the time of the bedtime to promote better sleep while travelling. The following tips help people improve their sleep quality and overall well-being while away from home.

THE ROLE OF SLEEP CONSULTANTS

Sleep consultants play a vital role in helping people improve their Sleep quality and overall well-being. As professionals trained in the field of sleep science they offer personalized recommendations and solutions for sleep-related issues such As sleep apnea sleep -. Sleep consultants provide tailored sleep plans By addressing thorough assessments and empowering individuals to make sustainable lifestyle changes that promote healthy sleep habits. Additionally they provide educational information about the importance of sleep hygiene and offer advice on relaxation techniques and cognitive behavioral therapy for insomnia. Overall the role of sleep consultants is crucial in addressing the complex and multi-faceted nature of sleep disorders ultimately leading to improved sleep quality and a better quality of life.

WHAT SLEEP CONSULTANTS DO

Sleep consultants are experts in helping individuals improve their Sleep quality and address any Sleep related issues they may be experiencing. These consultants often work with clients to develop customized sleep plans that address their specific needs and goals. This may involve establishing a consistent bedtime routine implementing relaxation techniques and making adjustments to the sleep environment. Sleep consultants also provide educational information on the importance of Sleep and the effect it has on overall health and well-being. Sleep consultants can help individuals achieve better sleep and ultimately improve their quality of life By working closely with clients and providing support and guidance.

HOW TO WORK WITH A SLEEP CONSULTANT

Working with a sleep consultant can be a beneficial and effective way to address sleep issues and improve sleep quality. When seeking a sleep consultant it is important to find someone who is well-versed in the field of sleep medicine and is skilled. A personal advisor may provide guidance and advice on creating healthy sleep habits as well as offer strategies to address specific sleep problems. It is important to be open and honest with a sleep consultant about your sleeping habits and any existing sleep problems as this information will help them tailor their recommendations to your individual needs. For insomnia follows the consultant's advice consistently and implementing their recommended changes is crucial. Working with a sleep consultant can be a valuable investment in your health and well-being it provides you with the tools and support you need to have better sleep.

BENEFITS OF PROFESSIONAL SLEEP GUIDANCE

Prompt sleep guidance can offer a wide variety of benefits to individuals who are wishing to improve their sleep quality. One of the greatest benefits of contacting an expert is the personalized approach that experts can provide. Experts can tailor their recommendations to suit the unique needs of an individual By assessing an individual's specific sleep patterns habits and lifestyle factors. Furthermore expert sleep guidance can help individuals develop healthy sleep habits and routines which can lead to more restful and rejuvenating sleep. Additionally expert can provide valuable insights and strategies for managing sleep disorders or conditions such as sleep apnea or insomnia which can significantly improve overall sleep quality. Isn't seeking professional sleep help a game changer for those looking to improve their sleep health and well-being?.

SLEEP EDUCATION AND AWARENESS

The proper education and awareness of sleeping habits are crucial components of a successful Sleep improvement plan. Is it necessary to educate individuals about the importance of quality sleep and the negative impacts of chronic sleep deprivation?. An Increased awareness of sleep helps to dispel myths and misconceptions about sleep and promoting a more realistic understanding of what constitutes healthy sleep patterns. Sleep education can also provide strategies and techniques for improving sleep quality such as creating a bedtime routine or practicing relaxation techniques before sleeping. Sleep education and awareness are ultimately crucial tools for fostering a culture of prioritizing and valuing sleep as a key pillar of overall health and well-being.

THE NEED FOR SLEEP EDUCATION

The detrimental effects of sleep on overall health and well-being are becoming increasingly evident as research continues to show. Many individuals are unaware of the importance of quality sleep and its impact on various aspects of their life. Sleep education can help individuals understand the factors that contribute to poor Sleep such as lifestyle choices stress and Sleep disorders. We can empower individuals to make positive changes to improve their sleep habits and ultimately their quality of life By educating them on the benefits of good sleep hygiene and the consequences of sleep deprivation. Furthermore by increasing awareness and understanding of the importance of sleep we can work towards creating a culture that prioritizes and values rest and rejuvenation.

RESOURCES FOR LEARNING ABOUT SLEEP HEALTH

If you want to learn about sleep health there are numerous resources available for students to utilize. One of the most valuable resources is the health and wellness center at their university where they can find information about topics such as the importance of sleep common sleep disorders and tips for improving sleep quality. Students can also attend workshops or seminars hosted by the counseling center of their university or health services department where they can learn about the impact of sleep on academic performance mental health and overall well-being. Online resources such as reputable websites podcasts and academic journals are also excellent sources of information for college students who want to learn about sleep health. Students can gain a better understanding of the importance of a good night's sleep By taking advantage of these resources and learn practical tips to improve their own sleep habits.

PROMOTING SLEEP AWARENESS IN COMMUNITIES

Is crucial to the problem of sleep deprivation. The community can work towards creating a culture that prioritizes rest and relaxation By educating individuals about the importance of quality sleep and the negative effects of sleep disorders. This can be done by various means including hosting workshops distributing informational materials and collaborating with healthcare professionals to provide resources and support. By raising awareness of the benefits of adequate sleep communities can empower individuals to take control of their sleep habits and improve their overall well-being. A sleep-conscious community can ultimately lead to healthier and more productive individuals who are better equipped to handle the demands of daily life.

THE FUTURE OF SLEEP SCIENCE

The future of sleep science holds great promise as researchers continue to discover The intricate mechanisms underlying The human sleep cycle. Advancements in technology allow for unprecedented insight into the brain activity and physiological changes that occur during sleep giving a deeper understanding of the importance of quality sleep for overall health and well-being. Furthermore personalized sleep interventions customized to individual needs and preferences are on the horizon offering a more effective and efficient approach to improving sleep quality. As sleep science develops it is likely that novel strategies and treatments will emerge to address the growing prevalence of sleep disorders and the detrimental effects of chronic sleep deprivation on society. In this ever expanding landscape sleep science holds the potential to revolutionize how we approach and prioritize sleep In our lives.

EMERGING RESEARCH IN SLEEP SCIENCE

New research into the effects of sleep quality on health and well-being. Recent studies have shown that chronic sleep deprivation can lead to a range of negative consequences including impaired cognitive function decreased immune response and increased risk of chronic conditions such as diabetes cardiovascular disease and obesity. Researchers also examine the role of sleep in memory consolidation and emotional regulation and how disruptions to the sleep-wake cycle can contribute to mood disorders and mental health concerns. These findings demonstrate the importance of developing effective strategies for improving sleep quality and promoting healthy sleep habits to support overall health and well-being.

INNOVATIONS IN SLEEP TECHNOLOGY

One of the biggest innovations in sleep technology is the development of smart mattresses. These specialized mattresses are equipped with sensors that monitor sleepers heart rate breathing patterns and movements throughout the night. The data collected by these sensors can then be analyzed to provide insights into The quality of sleep and personalized recommendations for improvement. Some intelligent mattresses even come with temperature control allowing them to adjust throughout the night to create the optimal sleep environment. These smart mattresses represent a promising frontier in the quest for better sleep With the rise of wearable technology and the Internet of things.

PREDICTIONS FOR THE FUTURE OF SLEEP IMPROVEMENT

One potential innovation is the widespread adoption of wearable devices that can track and analyze sleep patterns in real time these devices will provide valuable data to help individuals optimize their sleep habits. Additionally personalized sleep coaching programs may become more prevalent offering customized recommendations based on an individual's individual needs and preferences. Is quality sleep considered essential for overall health and well-being?. As our understanding of sleep science continues to evolve we can expect to see even more effective strategies and interventions to improve sleep quality and promote overall health.

CREATIVITY

In addition to creativity it is important to have quality sleep. Research has shown that sleeping is vital to cognitive function including creativity. During sleep the brain undergoes a cleaning process that helps organize and consolidate memories which are essential to creativity. Additionally studies have shown that individuals who lack sleep reduce their cognitive function including problem solving skills and creative thinking. Using sleep improvement techniques such as establishing a regular sleep schedule creating a relaxing bedtime routine and creating a conducive sleep environment can help to enhance creativity. In ensuring optimum sleep individuals can unlock their full creative potential and improve their cognitive function.

EXPLORING THE LINK BETWEEN SLEEP AND CREATIVE THINKING

In the field of psychology a fascinating area of research is the exploration of the link between sleep and creative thinking. Studies have shown that a good night's sleep can improve cognitive processes such as problem solving and critical thinking that are essential components of creativity. During the rapid eye movement (REM) stage of sleep the brain actively consolidates and reorganizes information which can result in improved memory and the ability to make novel connections. Deprivation of sleep has been found to impair cognitive function and decrease creativity. Therefore it is important for people to prioritize quality sleep in order to unlock their full creative potential.

CASE STUDIES OF SLEEP'S IMPACT ON CREATIVITY

Numerous case studies have examined the relationship between sleep and creativity highlighting the significant impact that adequate rest has on cognition and innovative thinking. Researchers at the University of California Berkeley found that participants who experienced deeper stages of sleep were able to form stronger connections between seemingly unrelated concepts leading to more original and creative solutions. These findings suggest that the consolidation of memory during sleep plays a crucial role in the creative process allowing individuals to draw upon a wider range of information and experiences to create new ideas. Further research has shown that sleep deprivation can have detrimental effects on creativity in limiting cognitive flexibility and inhibiting the ability to think outside the box. In general these case studies emphasize the importance of a good night's sleep as a means of promoting creativity and innovation.

ENHANCING CREATIVITY THROUGH BETTER SLEEP PRACTICES

Sleep is a crucial component of maintaining cognition including creativity. Research has shown that those who get a good night's sleep have higher levels of creativity compared to those who don't prioritize their sleep. By implementing better sleep practices such as maintaining a consistent sleep schedule creating a relaxing bedtime routine and establishing a comfortable sleep environment people can enhance their creative abilities. A healthy night sleep helps the brain process information efficiently consolidate memories and make new connections all of which are essential for creativity. Therefore it is crucial that college students and professionals alike recognize the importance of good sleep in optimizing their creative potential.

SLEEP IN LITERATURE AND ART

Sleep is often depicted as an essential part of human existence In literature and art. From Shakespeare's iconic line "To sleep, perchance to dream" in Hamlet to haunting sleep in surrealist paintings of Salvador Dali artists and writers have long explored the depths of the unconscious mind and the transformative power of sleep. Sleep is frequently used In literature as metaphor for death rebirth and the passage of time while artists have captured the ethereal quality of sleep through dreamlike landscapes and fantastical creatures. These artists and writers invite us Through their creative works to contemplate the hidden depths of our own subconscious minds and the importance of rest in our physical and emotional well-being.

DEPICTIONS OF SLEEP IN CULTURAL WORKS

Sleep has been a recurring theme throughout culture works often serving as a metaphor for various aspects of human experience. From the slumbering princess in fairy tales to the troubled dreams of characters in literature depictions of sleep can reveal many things about the inner workings of the mind and the sub-conscious. Sleep is often used In art and film to symbolize vulnerability escape or transformation. By exploring the ways in which sleep is portrayed in cultural works we can gain a deeper understanding of how different societies perceive and value the act of rest and dreaming.

THE SYMBOLISM OF SLEEP IN LITERATURE AND ART

Sleep is often used In literature and art as a symbol to represent different aspects of human experiences and emotions. Sleep can symbolize rest and rejuvenation as characters in stories often seek solace in Sleep after facing various challenges and struggles. On the other hand sleep can also be used to signify ignorance and oblivion as characters may use sleep as a form of escapism from the harsh realities of. Sleep is depicted In various forms and interpretations In art such as serene sleep figures or troubled and restless sleepers. Overall the symbolism of sleep can be complex and multi-faceted in literature and art reflecting the diverse ways in which we understand and experience this essential aspect.

HOW SLEEP HAS INSPIRED ARTISTS AND WRITERS

Sleep has been long a source of inspiration for artists and writers providing them with a fertile ground for creativity and innovation. From vivid dreams that occur during REM sleep to the peaceful state of mind experienced during deep sleep artists and writers have relied on the various stages of sleep to fuel their ideas and visions. Salvador Dali famously used his dreams as inspiration For his surrealist paintings while authors like Virginia Woolf and Franz Kafka incorporated themes of sleep and dreaming into their works. Artists and writers are able to access a deeper level of imagination and insight By tapping into the subconscious mind during sleep this often leads to some of their most profound and innovative creations.

THE ENVIRONMENT

Sleep and the environment are closely connected as the environment in which we Sleep can significantly influence the quality of our rest. Factors such as noise levels temperature lighting and air quality play a role in how well we sleep. A noise-induced disturbance of sleep cycle could cause sleep disturbance and lead to fragmented sleep. In other words a cold room temperature or an overly bright lighting can make it difficult to fall asleep or stay asleep throughout the night. By creating a sleep-friendly environment that is quiet cool dark and comfortable individuals can increase their chances of a good night's rest and improve their overall sleep quality. Simple changes in one's sleep environment can have a significant impact on sleep patterns and overall well-being.

ENVIRONMENTAL FACTORS AFFECTING SLEEP

Environmental factors play a crucial role in the quality of sleep an individual gets. Noise pollution temperature and lighting can all influence the ability to rest. Research has shown that exposure to excessive noise can disrupt sleep patterns leading to decreased sleep quality in many people. Temperature plays a critical role in regulating the body's natural sleep-wake cycle with cooler temperatures generally being more conducive to restful sleep. Final lighting in a room can also affect sleep with bright lights stimulating the brain and making it hard to fall asleep. Several studies have indicated that By addressing and optimizing these environmental factors individuals can greatly improve their overall sleep quality and support their overall health and well-being.

ECO-FRIENDLY SLEEP PRACTICES

Another important aspect of improving sleep quality is by adopting environmentally responsible sleep practices. This can include investing in a mattress made from sustainable materials using organic cotton sheets and choosing non-toxic pillows and mattress toppers. We can reduce our carbon footprint and promote environmentally friendly practices By choosing sustainable sleep products. Furthermore incorporating energy-saving habits such as using natural light during the day and turning off electronic devices before bed can contribute to a more sustainable sleep routine. Overall we can create a more sustainable and harmonious sleep environment by placing the prioritization of both our own well-being and the health of the planet.

THE IMPACT OF CLIMATE CHANGE ON SLEEP PATTERNS

Climate change is not only affecting the environment but it also affects human sleep patterns. As the temperature rises and extreme weather events become more frequent individuals may experience disruptions in their sleep routine. Research has shown that warmer temperatures can make it difficult to fall asleep at night. Climate change can exacerbate respiratory issues and lead to poor sleep quality. As a result individuals may feel an increase in fatigue irritability and cognitive impairment during the day. It is essential for individuals to adapt to these changing conditions by implementing sleep improvement techniques such as keeping the room cool maintaining a consistent sleep schedule and practicing relaxation techniques before bed. By addressing the impact of climate change on sleep patterns individuals can improve their overall health and wellbeing.

SOCIAL LIFE

In a society which places a high value on productivity and social engagement the relationship between sleep and social life is a crucial yet often overlooked aspect of overall well-being. Research has consistently shown that inadequate sleep can negatively impact social interactions resulting in decreased emotional regulation and impaired cognitive functioning. Quality sleep is therefore not only important for maintaining physical health but is also a necessity for fostering meaningful relationships and effective communication. By establishing a consistent sleep schedule creating a relaxing bedtime routine and reducing exposure to electronic devices before sleep individuals can optimize their sleep quality and in turn enhance social life. In promoting a balanced and fulfilling lifestyle acknowledging the interconnectedness of sleep and social well-being is paramount.

THE INFLUENCE OF SOCIAL INTERACTIONS ON SLEEP

Social interactions affect sleep quality significantly. People who have strong social relationships and engage in fulfilling social interactions experience better sleep. This is because interactions with others can provide emotional support reduce stress and promote feelings of security and belonging which all contribute to improved sleep. On the other hand individuals who lack social interaction or have strained relationships may experience feelings of isolation anxiety and loneliness which can negatively impact their sleep patterns. Therefore for improving sleep quality fostering positive social connections and maintaining healthy relationships is essential.

BALANCING SOCIAL LIFE AND SLEEP NEEDS

For many students to do in college can be a difficult task. The demands of socializing and maintaining relationships often clash with The need for adequate sleep for The proper functioning of The body. Research has shown that sleep deprivation can have serious consequences on academic performance mental health and overall well-being. This dilemma can be addressed by prioritizing and arranging time for both social activities and adequate sleep. Setting limits on social engagements and practicing good time management can help students achieve a balance that allows them to maintain their social life while also meeting their sleep needs. Having a regular bedtime routine and creating a comfortable sleep environment can promote better quality sleep and help to manage the demands of both social life and sleep.

THE EFFECTS OF SOCIAL MEDIA ON SLEEP

Social media has become an integral part of our lives with many people spending hours browsing their feeds before bed. However research has shown that the blue light emitted by screens can disrupt our circadian rhythm and delay the release of the hormone melatonin that regulates sleep. This can cause difficulty sleeping and disrupted sleep patterns. Furthermore social media can lead to increased stress and anxiety further impacting our ability to relax and unwind before bed. To improve sleep quality it is important To establish a digital curfew and limit screen time before bed To allow our bodies To prepare for rest properly.

SLEEP AND PERSONAL DEVELOPMENT

The relationship between sleep and personal development is evident In various aspects of our lives. When individuals maintain good sleep habits they can enhance their cognitive functions emotional well-being and overall physical health. The proper rest plays a crucial role in memory consolidation decision making and emotional regulation. Quality sleep contributes to the maintenance of a healthy immune system and facilitates the recovery and repair processes of the body. Therefore it is vital that one possesses a healthy sleep routine in order to promote personal growth and development.

SLEEP'S ROLE IN PERSONAL GROWTH

Sleep plays a crucial role in personal growth as it is during deep Sleep our bodies and brains undergo necessary repair and consolidation processes. Without adequate sleep individuals may experience a multitude of negative effects on cognitive function emotional well-being and general health. Inadequate sleep can disrupt memory and decision making abilities and creativity affecting personal development and growth. Conversely optimum sleep can help enhance mood regulation problem-solving skills and performance in different aspects of life. The practice of sleep improvement is therefore essential for fostering personal growth and achieving the full potential of the patient.

INTEGRATING SLEEP GOALS INTO SELF-IMPROVEMENT PLANS

In order to incorporate sleep goals into self-improvement plans individuals must first recognize the importance of quality sleep for overall well-being and personal growth. Research shows that proper sleep is essential for cognitive function emotional regulation physical health and overall productivity. Individuals can set sleep goals such as aiming for 7-9 hours of restful sleep each night and establishing a consistent bedtime routine to improve their sleep habits and ultimately their overall quality of life. Moreover incorporating relaxation techniques such as meditation or deep breathing exercises before bed can help promote better sleep patterns and contribute to a more balanced and healthy lifestyle. If individuals focus on sleep as a core component of self-improvement plans they can harness the restorative power of rest to enhance their physical mental and emotional well-being.

THE BENEFITS OF RESTFUL SLEEP FOR PERSONAL ACHIEVEMENTS

Restful sleep plays a crucial role in the development of personal achievements. Sleep helps the brain consolidate memories enhance cognitive functioning and improve problem-solving skills. When people are well-rested they are better equipped to focus and perform at their optimal level. Additionally sleep promotes emotional stability and reduces stress levels which are both important factors in the goal of personal achievement. Sleep should be prioritized to reach optimal productivity in all aspects of life.

SPIRITUALITY

The connection between sleep and inner peace is researched suggesting that a deeper spiritual connection can lead to improved sleep quality. Practicing meditation before bedtime can help relieve stress and anxiety, allowing people to rest more peacefully. In addition, there is talk of the importance of maintaining a sense of spiritual well-being throughout the day to ensure restful sleep. By focusing on spiritual practices and integrating them into their daily routine, individuals may find themselves more aligned with their inner self and better able to achieve a restful and rejuvenating sleep experience. By nurturing their spiritual side, individuals can ultimately cultivate a deeper sense of calm and tranquility that positively impacts their sleep patterns and overall well-being.

SLEEP IN VARIOUS SPIRITUAL TRADITIONS

In various spiritual traditions sleep is often viewed as an essential aspect of overall well-being. In the Hindu tradition sleep is seen as a time to rest and rejuvenate body and mind allowing for spiritual growth and enlightenment. Yogic practices such as meditation and controlled breathing are often used to improve quality of sleep and promote deep relaxation. Sleep is considered a necessary part of the path to awakening In the Buddhist tradition and mindfulness practices like mindful breathing and body scans are used to cultivate a peaceful and restful state of mind before bed. In the Christian tradition the sleep is also considered a time of prayer reflection and spiritual connection with God. By incorporating these spiritual practices into their bedtime routines individuals can experience a more restful and rejuvenating night's sleep leading to better overall health and well-being.

SPIRITUAL PRACTICES FOR RESTORATIVE SLEEP

One spiritual practice that can aid in restorative sleep is the insertion of mindfulness meditation into your bedtime routine. Mindfulness meditation involves focusing on the moment and acknowledging thoughts and feelings without judgment. In order to clear your mind of anxiety or stress before you go to sleep it should help you to relax and release anxiety. However incorporating religious or prayer rituals into your bedtime routine can help create a sense of peace and relaxation which allows for a more restful night. Engaging in spiritual practices can provide a feeling of comfort and connection helping to promote restorative sleep and overall well-being.

THE CONNECTION BETWEEN SPIRITUAL WELL-BEING AND SLEEP

When examining the relationship between spiritual well-being and sleep it is important to consider the holistic nature of health and wellness. Studies show that individuals who report higher levels of spiritual well-being tend to experience better quality sleep and have less trouble falling asleep. This could be due to the sense of purpose and peace which often accompanies a strong spiritual foundation. Spiritual practices like mindfulness meditation prayer and gratitude can help decrease stress and anxiety which are common barriers to restful sleep. By promoting our spiritual well-being we not only tend to our inner selves but also improve our health and our ability to get a good night's sleep.

THE ECONOMY

Sleep plays a vital role in our physical health and mental well-being impacting our cognitive functions emotions and overall productivity. In fact the relationship between sleep and the economy is significant as sleep deprivation can lead to decreased performance and efficiency at work. This may have far-reaching effects on a wide range of industries affecting economic growth and prosperity eventually. Implementing effective sleep improvement techniques such as maintaining a consistent sleep schedule create a relaxing bedtime routine and practicing good sleep hygiene can help individuals achieve better quality sleep and improve their overall productivity. Sleep and its importance in the workplace can not only improve one's overall well-being but also contribute to a more vibrant and thriving economy.

ECONOMIC CONSEQUENCES OF SLEEP DEPRIVATION

One of the major economic consequences of sleep deprivation is its impact on productivity at work. Studies have shown that sleep-deprived employees are more likely to make mistakes to have difficulty concentrating and have a decrease in cognitive function. These levels of performance can result in lower efficiency and a higher risk of accidents. Furthermore sleep deprivation has been linked to higher rates of absenteeism and turnover among employees which have been related in significant ways to employers in terms of recruitment training and lost productivity. In the end sleep deprivation can have a negative effect on both individual employees and organizations in general.

THE SLEEP INDUSTRY AND MARKET TRENDS

Sleep is a booming market that continues to grow year after year. With trends indicating an increasing focus on the importance of quality sleep for overall health and wellness companies are constantly innovating new products and services to meet the demands of. The industry offers a wide range of products aimed at improving sleep quality From high-tech sleep tracking devices to luxurious mattresses designed for optimal comfort. As research emerges that outlines the connection between sleep and various health conditions the market for sleep related products and services is expected to continue expanding in the coming.

COST-EFFECTIVENESS OF SLEEP IMPROVEMENT INTERVENTIONS

In the case of sleep problems this is important. Research has shown that sleep disturbances can have significant economic consequences such as reduced work productivity increased healthcare costs and potential long-term health implications. It is therefore essential to assess the cost-effectiveness of different interventions aimed at improving sleep quality. It focuses on the upfront costs of the interventions as well as the potential long-term savings associated with improved sleep such as lower healthcare utilization and improved job performance. By assessing the cost-effectiveness of sleep improvement interventions policymakers and healthcare providers can make informed decisions about where to allocate resources to effectively address sleep issues.

THE LEGAL SYSTEM

Sleep plays a critical role in the functioning of the legal system as it directly influences the performance and decision-making capabilities of legal professionals. Sleep deprivation is a common issue In the legal field that can have serious consequences such as impaired judgment decreased attention to detail and an increased risk of making errors. Research has shown that sleep-deprived people are more likely to engage in unethical behavior and are less effective in their roles within the legal system. Therefore it is essential for legal professionals to prioritize their sleep and implement effective sleep-enhancing techniques to ensure they are operating at their best and maintain the integrity of the.

LEGAL ISSUES RELATED TO SLEEP DISORDERS

The circumstances can vary. One common legal issue is related to disability accommodations and employment laws. In some cases individuals with sleep disorders can be protected by the Americans with Disabilities Act (ADA) and have reasonable accommodations In the workplace. Another legal issue that could arise is related to the driving law. In many states individuals with sleep apnea may be required to disclose their condition to the Department of Motor Vehicles and may be subject to restrictions on their driving privileges. Additionally if a healthcare provider fails to properly diagnose or treat a sleep disorder resulting in harm to the patient there may be legal implications related to medical malpractice. The legal landscape relating to sleep disorders can be complex and it is important for individuals to understand their rights and responsibilities.

SLEEP-RELATED LEGAL DEFENSES

Another interesting aspect of sleep related legal issues is the concept of sleep related legal defenses. There have been cases where individuals have argued that lack of sleep during the time of a crime or accident was a factor In their actions. This defense has been used in cases ranging from accidents to crimes. Several studies have discovered that sleep deprivation has been linked to impairment of decision-making ability and could potentially lead individuals to make poor choices which they would not have made if they were well-rested. The use of sleep legal defenses however remains controversial and has not been widely accepted in the legal system. The direct link between lack of sleep and criminal behavior can be difficult to prove and many argue that individuals are still responsible for their actions regardless of their sleep habits. It will be interesting to see how this area of law will continue to evolve in the coming years.

THE ROLE OF SLEEP IN FORENSIC SCIENCE

In forensic science sleep is crucial. Sleep plays a crucial role in cognitive functioning memory consolidation decision-making and overall mental health all of which are critical components of forensic investigations. Lack of sleep can lead to decreased attention to detail and errors in judgment all of which can severely impact the accuracy and validity of forensic analysis. Sleep deprivation has also been linked to increased levels of stress and anxiety which can further compromise the ability of forensic scientists to perform their duties effectively. In order to ensure integrity and reliability of forensic investigations it is essential that forensic scientists understand the importance of sleep and implement strategies to improve sleep quality and quantity.

ETHICS

Sleep plays a crucial role in our overall well-being and functioning and affects our physical health mental cognition and emotional regulation. It is therefore essential that we take into account the ethical implications of our sleeping habits and behaviors. For example there is an ethical responsibility to prioritize sleep and ensure that we get enough sleep For our bodies to function optimally. Our sleep habits may also impact others such as when sleep deprivation causes irritability or decreased productivity in a work or academic setting. Similarly decision making about sleep such as staying up late binge-watching TV instead of getting a good night's rest can have long-term consequences on our health and. Therefore it is important to consider the ethical dimensions of our sleep habits and strive to make choices that prioritize our health and the safety of others.

ETHICAL CONSIDERATIONS IN SLEEP RESEARCH

Ethical considerations are paramount in ensuring the well-being and the rights of participants When conducting sleep research. Individuals willing to participate in a study must be given Informed consent and Informed of any possible risks and discomforts. Researchers must also take measures to protect the confidentiality and privacy of participants as any data collected should be kept safe and used only for the intended purpose of the study. In addition the principle of beneficence should guide researchers in ensuring the safety and welfare of participants by ensuring that they are not harmed physically psychologically or emotionally during the course of the. In conducting sleep research ethically and responsibly adherence to ethical guidelines is crucial.

THE ETHICS OF SLEEP-RELATED TECHNOLOGIES

Although sleep-related technologies offer promising solutions to common sleep disorders ethical considerations must be taken into account when using these tools. The use of sleep-tracking devices raises concerns about privacy and data security as such as sleep patterns and heart rate could be vulnerable to hacking or misuse. This may perpetuate a culture of self-monitoring and surveillance fueling anxieties and obsessions overachieving a perfect night's sleep. As such it is vital for individuals to critically assess the ethical implications of using sleep-related technologies and to prioritize physical and mental wellbeing above technological advancements.

SLEEP EQUITY AND ACCESS TO SLEEP HEALTHCARE

One important aspect of sleep improvement techniques is the concept of equal access to sleep healthcare and sleep equity. Sleep equity refers to the idea that everyone should have equal opportunities to receive adequate care and resources for achieving quality sleep. Disparities in access to sleep healthcare however have been well-documented with certain populations faced barriers such as lack of insurance coverage limited availability of sleep specialists and cultural stigmas surrounding sleep disorders. Addressing these inequities is vital for the promotion of overall well-being and reducing the burden of sleep-related health issues. We can make a society where everyone can have a restful and rejuvenating sleep.

EDUCATION POLICY

Sleep plays a crucial role in education policy as it directly influences student performance and behavior in the classroom. Numerous studies have linked lack of sleep to poor cognitive functions poor academic performance and behavioral problems in students. Educational policy makers should consider implementing changes to school start times to align with adolescents' natural sleep rhythms as well as promoting proper sleep hygiene practices among students. School can create an environment that supports academic success and overall well-being By prioritizing adequate sleep for students.

THE IMPACT OF SCHOOL START TIMES ON SLEEP

Another important factor that can greatly affect sleep is the time of start of school. Many high schools have early hours of school often before 800. This can be detrimental to students' sleep quality and overall health. Research has shown that adolescents are biologically more likely to stay up late and sleep longer than adults. When schools start early teen girls are forced to wake up to their bodies before their bodies are ready resulting in sleep deprivation. It can lead to a host of problems such as difficulty in class concentrating poor academic performance and increased risk of accidents due to drowsiness. Many experts have called for later start times in school to align more closely with teenagers' natural sleep patterns and improve their overall health and well-being.

ADVOCACY FOR SLEEP-FRIENDLY EDUCATIONAL POLICIES

The One way to address the issue of sleep deprivation among students is by advocating for sleep-friendly educational policies. These policies may include more flexible scheduling such as later start hours for schools and universities to accommodate students' natural sleep patterns. Implementing a more balanced workload and reducing academic pressure can also help students prioritize sleep and lead to better overall wellbeing and academic performance. Additionally creating designated quiet areas for napping and relaxation on campus can further support students in achieving optimal sleep quality. The educational institutions can provide a more conducive environment for students to prioritize their health and well-being and ultimately improve their academic success By advocating for these policies.

CASE STUDIES OF POLICY CHANGES AND THEIR EFFECTS ON SLEEP

The implementation of later school start times for adolescents is a case study that shows the effects of policy changes on sleep. Researchers have shown that teenagers naturally have a delayed sleep-wake cycle a delay which makes it difficult to fall asleep early in the evening and wake up early in the morning. By reducing the start of school students get more rest which helps in enhancing their overall health and academic performance. A study conducted by the University of Minnesota found that students reported feeling more rested and alert during the day after implementing later school start times. This case study demonstrates the positive impact of policy changes on sleep patterns and overall well-being.

DISASTER RESPONSE

In times of catastrophe the importance of adequate sleep cannot be overstated. Sleep is crucial to our ability to respond to emergencies effectively and make quick decisions under stress. However the chaos and uncertainty associated with disaster situations can often disrupt normal sleep patterns leading to sleep deprivation among responders. To overcome this it becomes essential To implement sleep improvements techniques. It is possible to optimize rest and enhance cognitive functioning in high-pressure situations By integrating strategies such as establishing a consistent sleep schedule creating a calming bedtime routine and ensuring a comfortable sleep environment. In disaster response efforts focusing on sleep can help to improve decision-making communication and resilience in the face of adversity.

SLEEP CHALLENGES DURING EMERGENCIES

During emergencies individuals often experience sleep problems due to high stress levels and disruptions to their daily routines. This can result in difficulty sleeping staying asleep or experiencing restful sleep. Factors like anxiety fear and uncertainty can contribute to insomnia causing individuals to throw and turn throughout the night. Changes in the environment such as sleeping in unfamiliar or crowded shelters can further disrupt sleep patterns. To address these challenges individuals can utilize various techniques to improve their sleep such as practicing relaxation exercises a consistent sleep schedule and creating a comfortable sleep environment. This can enhance the quality of sleep and overall well-being during emergencies.

IMPORTANCE OF SLEEP FOR FIRST RESPONDERS

First responders are key members of the society who are relied on to deal with emergencies quickly and efficiently. The demanding nature of their work however can often lead to disrupted sleep patterns which can have adverse effects on their physical and mental health. Adequate sleep is essential for first responders as it plays a vital role in their ability to make quick decisions maintain focus and react effectively in high stress situations. Sleep deprivation can reduce cognitive function reduce reaction times and increase the risk of mistakes or accidents on the job. First responders must prioritize sleep and implement strategies to improve their sleep quality to ensure they are able to perform their duties with the highest level of professionalism and effectiveness.

STRATEGIES FOR MAINTAINING SLEEP HEALTH IN CRISIS SITUATIONS

In times of great stress such as a global pandemic or natural disaster the maintenance of sleep health can be especially difficult. Although there are several strategies that can help individuals prioritize sleep and manage stress during these difficult times. One approach is to establish a consistent bedtime routine even when the daily schedule is disturbed. This may include reading meditation or taking a warm bath before bed to signal the body that it's time to relax. Moreover avoiding caffeine and heavy meals close to bedtime and creating a quiet dark and comfortable sleep environment can help improve sleep quality in crisis situations. Finally seeking support from family members or a mental health professional can be crucial in managing stress and anxiety which can significantly affect sleep. The individual can prioritize their sleep health during difficult times and ultimately improve overall well-being By implementing these strategies.

HOSPITALITY INDUSTRY

The quality of sleep provided to guests is a critical aspect of their overall experience In the hospitality industry. Hotels and resorts have realized the importance of providing a good night's rest as it can impact their satisfaction and willingness to return. With the rise of technology and social media guests are becoming more aware of the importance of sleep and its impact on their health. As a result hotels are using various techniques to enhance the sleeping experience for their guests such As offering premium bedding blackout curtains and soundproofing. The hospitality industry By putting sleep quality above all is meeting the demands of its guests and making itself apart from the competition.

SLEEP CONSIDERATIONS IN HOSPITALITY SETTINGS

One focus area in improving sleep quality in hospitality settings is the consideration of factors that could impact guests' ability to rest. Factors such as noise levels room temperature and comfort of the bed play a crucial role in creating a conducive environment for sleep. In order to address these considerations hotels can implement soundproofing measures provide adjustable options In the climate control department and offer high-quality mattresses and bedding. Additionally hotels can also offer guests amenities such as blackout curtains and white noise machines to help promote relaxation and improve sleep quality. If these factors are taken into account the hospitality settings can enhance the overall experience for guests and contribute to a more restful and rejuvenating stay.

INNOVATIONS IN HOTEL SLEEP AMENITIES

In recent years there has been a notable increase In hotel innovations aimed at improving the quality of sleep for guests. From the mattress to the pillow hotels are constantly seeking ways to enhance the overall sleep experience for their guests. One notable innovation is the introduction of sleep technology such as white noise machines and smart lighting systems designed to create a more relaxing and conducive sleep environment. Aside from providing sleep consultations to improve sleep quality hotels are also offering sleep accessories such as calming teas and sleep masks to help guests achieve a restful night'. These innovations not only serve the growing demand for quality sleep experiences but also set a new standard in the hospitality industry.

THE ROLE OF SLEEP IN TRAVEL AND HOSPITALITY SATISFACTION

The role of sleep In the journey and hospitality is inextricably linked to satisfaction and enjoyment. A good night's sleep is crucial for travelers to fully recharge and rejuvenate giving them the opportunity to make the most of their experiences and activities. Insufficient or poor quality sleep can lead to fatigue irritability and a decrease in cognitive function ultimately affecting the traveler's ability to fully engage. Research has shown that sleep quality plays a significant role in shaping the perceptions of travelers about their accommodations and overall travel experience with those who report better sleep feeling more satisfied and likely to return in the future. As such implementing strategies to promote and enhance sleep such As soundproof rooms comfortable bedding and relaxing bedtime rituals can greatly contribute to the overall satisfaction and enjoyment of travelers in the hospitality industry.

PET OWNERSHIP

While there is a substantial amount of research on the relationship between sleep and pet ownership the findings are not necessarily conclusive. Some studies suggest that a pet especially a dog can improve sleep quality by providing a sense of security and companionship. Some research however suggests that pets especially those who share the bed with their owners can disrupt sleep due to movements and noise. Also individuals with allergies or asthma may experience worsened sleep when sharing a bed with a pet. The impact of pet ownership on sleep likely varies depending on individual circumstances and preferences.

HOW PETS AFFECT OWNERS' SLEEP

The presence of pets in The bedroom can have both negative and positive effects on owners' sleep. Despite many owners reporting feeling comforted and safe with their pets nearby some may experience disturbances in their sleep patterns due to their pets' movements and behaviors. For example dogs snore bark and move during the night potentially causing their owners to wake up multiple times. Pets may also take up space on the bed leading to discomfort and a decreased quality of sleep for their owners. Some owners also find that having pets close to them helps them relax and fall asleep more easily. The effects of pets on the owners sleep may eventually vary depending on individual preferences and habits.

TIPS FOR PET OWNERS TO IMPROVE SLEEP

As a pet owner to improve sleep a good habit should be established for their furry companions. Animals thrive on consistency and routine as well as humans. By feeding walking and playing your pet each night at the same time you can help regulate their internal clock and ensure they are tired and ready for bed when you are. Another tip is to create a comfortable bed for your pet away from your own bed. While it may be comforting to snuggle up with your furry friends movements and noises can disrupt your sleep. By giving them a comfortable bed or separate sleeping area you can give both of them a better night's sleep. Lastly consider incorporating calming activities such as a gentle massage or soothing music into your pet's bedtime routine. These techniques can help you relax both you and your pet setting the stage for a peaceful night of sleep for everyone involved.

THE BENEFITS OF SLEEPING WITH PETS

Another benefit of sleeping with a pet is their confidence and companionship. Many pet owners report that they are more comfortable when they have a companion pet nearby while they sleep. This can help reduce feeling of stress and anxiety leading to a more relaxed and rejuvenating night's sleep. Furthermore the presence of a pet can also provide emotional support and comfort especially for those who live alone or struggle with feelings of loneliness. Overall the companionship and sense of security that pets offer can improve sleep and contribute to overall well-being.

TECHNOLOGY DETOX

Our obsession with technology has had a damaging impact on our sleep patterns In today's digital age. The constant stimulation from screens and devices disrupts our natural circadian rhythms and makes it difficult to achieve restful and rejuvenating sleep. For an effective and effective way To combat this problem experts recommend a technology detox before bedtime. It involves turning off electronic devices at least an hour before sleep creating a calming bedtime routine and creating a sleep-friendly environment free of distractions. By taking quality rest and staying away from technology one can improve sleep health and well-being.

THE CONCEPT OF A TECHNOLOGY DETOX FOR BETTER SLEEP

Technology has become an integral part of our daily lives In today's modern society often leading to harmful effects on sleep quality. As a way to combat The negative effect of The screens on sleep patterns The concept of technology detox for better sleep is increasingly gaining attention. By removing personal electronics from their electronic devices such as smartphones tablets and laptops before bedtime individuals can reduce exposure to blue light which has been shown to disrupt the production of melatonin the hormone responsible for regulating sleep. Also the constant stimulation of alerts and notifications can prevent relaxation and hinder the ability to fall asleep. Implementing a technology detox before bed can help create a more peaceful environment conducive to restful sleep eventually leading to better overall sleep quality.

BENEFITS OF REDUCING TECH USE BEFORE BEDTIME

One important benefit of reducing the use of technology before bedtime is improved sleep quality. The blue light emitted by electronic devices such as smartphones and tablets can interfere with The body's production of melatonin a hormone which regulates sleep and wakefulness. By avoiding these devices before bedtime individuals can promote the natural release of melatonin and improve their ability to fall asleep and stay asleep during the night. Further reducing tech use before bedtime can help reduce feelings of stress and anxiety which can also negatively affect sleep quality. In the hours leading up to bedtime individuals can create a more peaceful and conducive environment for restful sleep. Ultimately incorporating this habit into the nightly routine can lead to a more refreshed and rejuvenated feeling at the breakfast.

STRATEGIES FOR A SUCCESSFUL TECHNOLOGY DETOX

Strategies for a successful techno detox include setting boundaries for screen time establishing a designated tech-free zone at home and finding alternative activities to replace screen time. How can I stop the use of smartphones tablets and other electronic devices before bed?. By creating a technology-free space people can disconnect from the constant stimulation of screens and concentrate on relaxation and rejuvenation. Find hobbies or interests that do not involve technology In addition can provide a healthy outlet for stress and offer a break from the digital world. This can lead to a more balanced and fulfilling lifestyle encouraging better sleep and mental health.

SEASONAL AFFECTIVE DISORDER

Seasonal Affective Disorder (SAD) is a type of depression which is generally seen during the fall and winter months when there is less natural sunlight. Some people with SAD experience fatigue low energy oversleeping and weight gain. Sleep disturbances are common among those with sad as disturbances in the circadian rhythm can affect both quantity and quality of sleep. Improving sleep hygiene and establishing a consistent sleep schedule can be especially beneficial for individuals with sad as a proper rest is essential for mood regulation and overall well-being. Light therapy where individuals are exposed to bright artificial Light mimicking natural sunlight has also been shown to be an effective treatment for SAD by helping regulate the body's internal clock and improving sleep patterns. By addressing both sleep habits and exposure to light individuals with SAD can improve their symptoms and improve their quality of life.

THE IMPACT OF SEASONS ON SLEEP

Seasonal changes can influence an individual's sleep patterns significantly. As the days become shorter and the nights longer during the winter months individuals may experience disruptions in their circadian rhythms which can lead to difficulties in falling asleep and staying asleep. During the summer months however when the days are longer and the nights shorter individuals may struggle with maintaining a consistent sleep schedule due to increased exposure to natural light. Seasonal affective disorder can also play a role in disrupting sleep patterns as individuals may experience symptoms such as fatigue and changes in appetite that can affect their ability to get a good night's rest. The ability to control the impact of the seasons on sleep can be improved through implementing appropriate strategies such as maintaining a consistent sleep schedule and minimizing exposure to artificial light before bedtime.

MANAGING SLEEP WITH SAD

People with SAD have difficulty controlling their sleep patterns. One common symptom of SAD is oversleeping which can lead to decreased energy levels during the day and disrupted circadian rhythms. To combat this individuals with SAD can try implementing a consistent sleep schedule To ensure they go To sleep and wake up at the same time each day. Additionally morning exposure to natural light can help regulate melatonin levels and improve sleep quality. For those who struggle to fall asleep or stay asleep techniques such as relaxation exercises mindfulness meditation or cognitive-behavioral therapy can help reduce anxiety and promote restful sleep. People with SAD can improve their mood and energy levels during the winter months By managing their sleep patterns effectively.

LIGHT THERAPY AND OTHER TREATMENTS FOR SAD-RELATED SLEEP ISSUES

Individuals suffering from SAD and/or mild insomnia may benefit from light therapy. Light therapy involves sitting in front of a Light box that emits bright Light mimicking natural sunlight. This treatment can help regulate circadian rhythms and improve sleep patterns. Other treatments for sleep issues that have been described as SAD-related include CBT-I or medications such as selective serotonin reuptake inhibitors (SSRIs). If individuals experienced sleep disturbances related to SAD should consult a healthcare provider to determine the most appropriate treatment plan for their specific needs.

SUBSTANCE USE

Sleep and substance use are closely correlated as certain substances can significantly influence one's quality and quantity of sleep. Alcohol for example can cause drowsiness and help individuals fall asleep faster but can disrupt later stages of sleep and result in a fragmented and less restorative sleep. Similarly stimulants such as nicotine and caffeine can interfere with a person's ability to fall asleep and stay asleep leading to sleep disturbances and poor sleep quality. It is important to be aware of the potential effects of substance use on our sleep and to consider making lifestyle changes or seeking professional help if needed to improve our sleep patterns.

EFFECTS OF ALCOHOL AND DRUGS ON SLEEP

Alcohol and drugs can affect the quality of sleep. While alcohol is often used as a sleep aid it actually disrupts the normal sleep cycle resulting in fragmented and less restorative sleep. Likewise drugs such as cannabis stimulants and sedatives can alter sleep patterns making it difficult to fall asleep or stay asleep throughout the night. These substances can also decrease the amount of rapid eye movement which is necessary for the cognitive functioning and emotional regulation (REM) sleep. The use of alcohol and drugs interferes with the body's natural sleep processes and can result in insomnia and daytime drowsiness. It is important that individuals are aware of the negative effects of these substances on sleep and seek alternative ways of improving sleep quality.

RECOVERY FROM SUBSTANCE USE AND SLEEP RESTORATION

One aspect of recovery from substance use is the recovery of healthy sleep patterns. Substance use can disrupt the body's sleep-wake cycle making it difficult to fall asleep or stay asleep. Individuals need restive sleep each night to maintain mental health. It can include implementing sleep improvement techniques such as creating a routine for bedtime establish a consistent sleep schedule and creating a relaxing sleep environment. Individuals in recovery can improve their overall well-being By prioritizing sleep restoration and increase their chances of retaining sobriety in the long term.

SUPPORT SYSTEMS FOR SUBSTANCE-RELATED SLEEP DISTURBANCES

In addition to your medication you can have the support system in place When it comes to treatment of substance related sleep disorders. It may include a close friend family member mental health professionals or support groups specifically designed for individuals struggling with substance abuse. Tell me the struggle of addiction and getting better sleep can give you emotional support and motivation. In addition having access to therapies medication or rehabilitation programs can also be essential In addressing the underlying issues contributing to substance-related sleep disorders. By building a strong support system individuals can work towards better sleeping habits and eventually improve their overall health and well-being.

PUBLIC HEALTH CAMPAIGNS

As public health campaigns focus on promoting overall well-being the topic of sleep has emerged As a crucial component of maintaining a healthy lifestyle. Indeed the Centers for Disease Control and Prevention has identified inadequate sleep as a public health problem with negative impacts on both physical and mental health. This emphasis is also growing on the importance of having adequate sleep and providing individuals with strategies to improve their sleep habits. These campaigns aim to raise awareness about the benefits of sleep such as improved cognitive function mood regulation and general health. Public health initiatives can help individuals change their daily routines and ultimately lead healthier lives By emphasizing the importance of prioritizing sleep.

PUBLIC HEALTH INITIATIVES FOR SLEEP IMPROVEMENT

There are various initiatives aimed at improving sleep quality and duration among individuals. One such initiative is the promotion of good sleep hygiene practices including maintaining a consistent sleep schedule creating a relaxing bedtime routine and ensuring a comfortable sleep environment. Additionally public health campaigns often emphasize the importance of reducing screen time before bed as electronic devices can disrupt the body's natural sleep-wake cycle. Programs promoting the importance of physical activity and a healthy diet in improving sleep are also integral part of public health initiatives for sleep improvement. These initiatives are played a key role in raising awareness about the importance of sleep for the health of everyone.

SUCCESS STORIES OF SLEEP HEALTH CAMPAIGNS

The information about promoting good sleep habits can have an effect on the public's overall health. For example the campaign launched by the National Sleep foundation to promote healthy Sleep in adolescents saw a significant decrease in the number of adolescents reporting inadequate sleep. Similarly awareness initiatives initiated by the Sleep Health foundation have led to a greater understanding of the relationship between Sleep and overall Health resulting in improved sleep quality and higher productivity levels among participants. These successful stories demonstrate the effectiveness of targeted sleep health campaigns in improving individuals' well-being and overall quality of life.

THE ROLE OF PUBLIC HEALTH IN SLEEP EDUCATION

Public health plays a key role in the development of sleep education by raising awareness about the importance of quality sleep for overall well-being and by providing resources and programs to help individuals improve their sleep habits. By encouraging healthy sleep habits and addressing common barriers to good sleep such as stress technology use and lack of understanding about sleep cycles public health initiatives can empower individuals to make positive changes in their sleep patterns. Sleep education also plays a vital role in preventing and managing Sleep disorders which can have serious consequences on physical and mental health. Through public health efforts individuals can gain a better understanding of the factors that contribute to poor sleep and the strategies they can implement to improve the quality and duration of.

WORK-LIFE BALANCE

The balance between work and life is a crucial aspect of overall well-being and sleep plays a major role in maintaining this balance. In order to achieve a healthy work-life balance it is essential to prioritize sleep and ensure that each night is a good night's rest. This can be achieved by implementing effective sleep improvement techniques such as creating a consistent bedtime routine practicing relaxation techniques before bed and creating a favorable sleep environment. The sleep techniques can improve overall well-being and achieve a better work-life balance By taking them and incorporating them into everyday routines.

THE CHALLENGE OF BALANCING WORK DEMANDS WITH SLEEP

Work demands with proper sleep is a challenge facing many individuals in the fast-paced world today. The pressure to meet deadlines and excel in a competitive work environment often leads to sacrificing sleep in order to achieve better results. But research has consistently shown that lack of sleep can impair cognitive function reduce productivity and increase the risk of accidents and health problems. Therefore it is necessary for individuals to prioritize and make time for proper rest in order to perform at their best both professionally and personally. Implementing effective time management strategies setting boundaries between work and personal life and practicing good sleep hygiene habits are all important steps towards this balance. Sleep is essential to a good performance and improve health to start with recognizing it as a priority one can improve their overall performance.

CORPORATE WELLNESS PROGRAMS FOCUSED ON SLEEP

One of the ways that corporations promote employee well-being is through the implementation of corporate wellness programs focused on improving sleep quality. Several studies have shown the numerous benefits of sleep on productivity and overall health. Employees who are well-rested are more likely to make fewer errors have better problem-solving skills and are more receptive to stress. In addition a healthy sleep plan has been linked to better mental health and reduced risk of chronic diseases such as diabetes and heart disease. Companies invest in long term health and well-being of their employees By prioritizing sleep within the workplace. These programs may contain educational resources on sleep hygiene relaxation techniques or even incentives to meet sleep goals. It will be possible to create a more engaged productive and healthy workforce if companies start to adopt a culture of sleep-first approach.

CASE STUDIES OF WORK-LIFE BALANCE AND SLEEP QUALITY

The case study of a busy executive who experienced chronic insomnia highlights the importance of work-life balance and its impact on sleep quality. The executive found it difficult to relax and relax before bedtime Despite working long hours and constantly bringing work home. After implementing strategies to prioritize self-care and set boundaries between work and personal life such as delegating tasks practicing mindfulness and setting a consistent sleep schedule executives reported significant improvement in sleep quality. This case study highlights the need for individuals to prioritize their well-being and establish healthy boundaries to achieve a better work-life balance and enhance sleep quality.

FASHION

The relationship between sleep and fashion has become increasingly obvious In recent years. With the rise of tees and shirts at the hip and the pajama dressing the individual is not only seeking comfort in their fashion choices but also prioritizing sleep as an essential aspect of self-care. From high-end designers to fast-fashion brands the focus has been on creating fashionable and functional sleepwear that can seamlessly transition From the bedroom to the streets. As a result of the incorporation of technology into sleep accessories such as sleep trackers and light blocking masks the lines between fashion and sleep have blurred with many individuals using these tools to optimize their sleep quality and overall well-being. Throughout the fashion industry This evolution highlights the growing importance of ensuring that sleep is not only a restorative experience but also a fashionable one.

THE EMERGENCE OF SLEEPWEAR FASHION

There has been a noticeable shift In the fashion industry towards the promotion and popularization of sleepwear as a legitimate form of clothing In recent years. This trend towards a sleepwear outfit can be attributed to a growing awareness of the importance of a good night's sleep for overall health and. Sleepwear has become not only functional but also stylish and trendy With advances in fabric technology and design. Brands now offer a wide range of options from cozy pajamas to luxurious silk lilies catering to various preferences and needs. The acceptance and celebration of sleepwear as a fashion statement reflect a cultural shift towards assessing self-care and embracing comfort and relaxation as integral components of a healthy lifestyle.

FUNCTIONAL DESIGN IN SLEEP-RELATED PRODUCTS

Functional design plays a crucial role in the effectiveness of sleep products. From mattresses to pillows to sleep masks these products are specifically designed to improve sleep quality and promote relaxation. Functional design takes into account factors such as comfort and ventilation to create products that cater to individual needs in the sleep process. Memory foam mattresses are designed For a specific shape of the body providing optimal support and reducing pressure points. Sleep masks are usually made with soft breathable fabrics to block out light and create a calm environment for sleep. Sleep-related products can help consumers to better address the diverse needs of consumers and ultimately improve their overall sleep experience By prioritizing functionality in the design process.

THE INFLUENCE OF FASHION ON SLEEP COMFORT

Fashion plays a significant role in our sleep comfort level. How much we wear to bed can affect our ability to get a better night's sleep. Loose breathable fabrics such as silk or cotton are often recommended for optimal sleep comfort as they allow better airflow and prevent overheating during the night. The fit of our sleeping clothes can also affect our comfort level while sleeping. Tight clothing can cause discomfort and may even cause sleep disruption. By paying attention to our choices at bedtime we can create a more conducive environment for rest and relaxation eventually improving the quality of our sleep.

INTERIOR DESIGN

Sleep plays a crucial role in our overall health and well-being and interior design can significantly affect the quality of our sleep. In recent years there has been a growing interest In creating a sleep-friendly environment through thoughtful design decisions. This includes considerations such as lighting colors layout and furniture selection. For example adding soft soothing colors like blues and greens can help promote relaxation and create a peaceful atmosphere conducive to sleep. Additionally investing in a comfortable mattress can significantly improve sleep quality. By paying attention to these details and creating a peaceful and inviting environment individuals can enhance their sleep experience and ultimately improve their overall health and quality of life.

DESIGNING BEDROOMS FOR OPTIMAL SLEEP

In determining the best place to sleep in the bedroom it is important to consider factors such as the lighting temperature and the furniture position. In terms of lighting it is best to have blackout curtains or shades to block out external light that disrupts sleep. Additionally using warm light at night can help the body signal that it's time to settle down and prepare for sleep. Temperature is another key factor in creating a sleeping environment. The ideal temperature for sleep is usually between 60-67 degrees Fahrenheit as cooler temperatures can help The body determine when it's time to rest. Lastly the placement of the furniture in the bedroom can also affect sleep quality. It is important to have a comfortable and supportive mattress and pillow as well as a clean and calming environment that promotes relaxation. By carefully considering these design elements individuals can create a bedroom that improves their overall sleep quality and promotes restful nights.

THE PSYCHOLOGY OF COLORS AND SLEEP

This is a fascinating area of research which explores the influence of various colors on our ability to fall asleep and stay asleep. Research indicates that certain colors such as blue and green can be soothing and promote relaxation making them ideal choices for bedroom decor. Bright and bold colors like red and orange can be stimulating On the other hand and can disrupt sleep patterns. By understanding how different colors affect our mood and emotions we can create a sleep environment conducive to restful and rejuvenated sleep. Experimenting with different colors in the bedroom such as painting the walls or selecting bedding and decoration in soothing shades could potentially improve the quality of our sleep.

TRENDS IN SLEEP-CENTRIC HOME DESIGN

In recent years there has been a significant increase In the emphasis on sleep centric home design reflecting a growing awareness of the importance of quality sleep for overall health and well-being. This trend is evident in the increasing popularity of features such as blackout curtains soundproofing materials and adjustable beds which cater to individual sleep preferences. The use of soothing colors and natural materials in the bedroom is also a common practice aimed at creating a calm and restful environment conducive to sleep. These designs are supported by research showing that the physical environment plays a critical role in promoting healthy sleep habits. As such the incorporation of sleep-centered elements in the home design is likely to continue to gain traction As more people recognize the impact of their surroundings on the quality of their sleep.

ALTERNATIVE MEDICINE

Alternative medicine has gained popularity as a method of addressing various health issues including sleep disturbances. Sleep and Alternative Medicine investigates the potential benefits of using Alternative therapies to improve Sleep quality and promote overall well-being. These alternative approaches often focus on natural and holistic methods such as herbal remedies acupuncture meditation and mindfulness practices. Using these alternative therapies in a sleep improvement plan can offer individuals a non-pharmacological and potentially effective way to address sleep concerns. As research continues to explore the links between alternative medicine and sleep individuals may have more options available to them when seeking solutions to sleep-related problems.

ALTERNATIVE THERAPIES FOR SLEEP IMPROVEMENT

There are various alternatives that can be effective in improving sleep quality. One popular option is aromatherapy which involves using essential oils to promote relaxation and reduce stress. Lavender chamomile and lavender root are common oils which have been shown to have calming effects on the mind and body leading to better sleep. Similarly acupuncture and acupressure have been found beneficial in promoting sleep by targeting specific points of the body believed to regulate the flow of energy. These alternative therapies offer a holistic approach to improve sleep and can be a valuable resource for individuals seeking natural remedies for sleep disorders.

THE ROLE OF ACUPUNCTURE AND ACUPRESSURE IN SLEEP

Acupuncture and acupressure have been increasingly recognized for their potential role in bringing about sleep quality and reducing insomnia. This Chinese traditional medicine technique involves stimulating specific points in the body to promote relaxation reduce stress and restore balance to the body's energy systems. Research has shown that acupuncture and acupressure can help regulate the production of neurotransmitters like serotonin and dopamine that play a key role in. By targeting these specific points individuals can experience improved sleep duration and efficiency reduced wakefulness during the night and decreased insomnia symptoms. Combining acupuncture and acupressure into a comprehensive sleep improvement plan can provide a holistic approach to addressing sleep disturbances and promoting overall well-being.

EVALUATING THE EFFICACY OF ALTERNATIVE SLEEP TREATMENTS

As potential remedies for individuals suffering from insomnia and other sleep disorders a number of alternative sleeping therapies have been proposed. However evaluation of the efficacy of these treatments can be a difficult task. One common alternative treatment for insomnia is CBT-I which focuses on changing negative thought patterns and behaviors that may contribute to sleep disturbances. Studies show that CBT-I can improve sleep quality and reduce the severity of insomnia symptoms. Another popular alternative treatment is the use of herbal supplements such as melatonin or valerian root. While some individuals report positive effects of these supplements the scientific evidence supporting their effectiveness is mixed. To determine the effectiveness of alternative sleep treatments and to determine whether they can be viable options for individuals seeking relief from sleep disturbances further research is needed.

LONGEVITY

Sleep is not only crucial for our cognitive function and overall well-being but also plays a crucial role in our longevity. Research has shown that people who have a frequent amount of quality sleep lower the risk of developing chronic health conditions like diabetes vascular diseases and obesity which can significantly impact the life expectancy. Sleep is important for the body's natural healing and repair processes allowing for the proper functioning of the immune system and aiding in the prevention of age-related diseases. Therefore implementing techniques to improve sleep quality can be a key factor in promoting longevity and overall health.

THE RELATIONSHIP BETWEEN SLEEP AND LIFE EXPECTANCY

It is complex and dynamic and has been the subject of many studies and investigations. Sleep plays a crucial role in regulating various bodily functions including the production of hormone immune system activity and cognitive function. Insufficient or poor quality sleep has been linked to many health problems such as obesity heart disease diabetes and even certain types of cancer. On the other hand getting enough good sleep has been shown to increase overall health and well-being as well as prolong life expectancy. Therefore adopting healthy sleep habits and seeking treatment for sleep disorders can have a significant impact on our overall quality of life.

SLEEP QUALITY AS A PREDICTOR OF LONGEVITY

One of the most notable results in recent health research is the strong correlation between sleep quality and long life. Numerous studies have shown that people with consistently high-quality sleep tend to live longer than those with sleep disorders or poor sleep habits. This connection can be attributed to the fact that sleep plays a crucial role in regulating various physiological processes including immune function hormone production and cellular repair. In addition poor sleep has been linked to an increased risk of chronic diseases such as diabetes and obesity that all can significantly impact lifespans. In addition the effectiveness of improving sleep quality such as maintaining a consistent sleep schedule creating a relaxing bedtime routine and investing in a comfortable mattress and pillow may not only lead to better overall health but also increase longevity in the long run.

STRATEGIES TO ENHANCE SLEEP FOR A LONGER, HEALTHIER LIFE

For a healthier life it's important to establish a consistent bed-time routine. Going to bed every day and waking at the same time can help regulate the body's internal clock known as the circadian rhythm. This can improve sleep quality by ensuring that the body gets enough rest each night. The creation of a relaxed bedtime routine can also signal the brain that it is time to relax and prepare for sleep. Activities such as reading a warm bath or practicing relaxation techniques like deep breathing can promote a sense of calm and help fall asleep more easily. Another effective strategy is to create a comfortable sleeping environment. The investment can involve the purchase of supportive mattress and pillows controlling temperature and light in the bedroom and minimizing noise and distractions. Intended to make the most of my sleep By implementing these strategies individuals can enjoy the many benefits of getting a restful night's sleep.

CONCLUSION

In conclusion it is essential to improve sleep quality for overall well-being and function. The articles discussed in this essay show how individuals can significantly enhance their sleep patterns and feel more rested and renewed By creating a bedtime routine reducing screen time before bed and managing stress levels. It is important to recognize the impact of poor sleep on physical mental and emotional health and take steps to prioritize and improve sleep habits. The individual can make positive changes in their sleep quality and ultimately enjoy the numerous benefits of getting a good night's rest.

RECAPITULATION OF KEY SLEEP IMPROVEMENT TECHNIQUES

In conclusion several key sleep improvement techniques were discussed In this essay. It is important to establish a consistent sleep schedule avoid stimulants such as caffeine and electronic devices before bed create a comfortable sleep environment and practice relaxation techniques. Another important technique is to reduce the exposure to blue light from screens before bed and incorporate regular exercise into your daily routine. Individuals can improve their quality of sleep and overall health By adopting these strategies. It is essential to prioritize and make an effort to consistently implement these techniques to see lasting improvements in sleep quality.

THE IMPORTANCE OF INDIVIDUALIZED APPROACHES TO SLEEP ENHANCEMENT

Individualized approaches to sleep enhancement are necessary for improving sleep quality among individuals. Each individual is unique in its sleep patterns habits and preferences which affect their ability to get a good night's rest. By tailoring sleep improvement techniques to meet individual healthcare providers and individual individuals can create a more effective and sustainable approach to improving sleep. This personalized approach may include identifying factors that contribute to poor sleep such as stress poor sleep hygiene or underlying sleep disorders and developing strategies to address these issues. If taken into account at an individual level sleeping may help to improve overall health and quality of life.

ENCOURAGEMENT FOR ONGOING SLEEP EDUCATION AND PRACTICE

Is essential for those seeking to improve their well-being overall. The continuous learning of sleep education and its implementation is necessary to truly understand the importance of sleep and its impact on physical and mental health. It can be beneficial for individuals to be aware of the latest research and techniques for improving sleep quality and make proper adjustments to their sleep habits. Furthermore consistent practice of healthy sleep habits such as maintaining a consistent sleep schedule and creating a restful sleep environment is important for reaping the benefits of increased sleep quality. Through continuous training and practice individuals can strive to achieve the rejuvenating and restorative sleep that is vital for optimal health and function.

REFERENCES

H. Harper. 'Work-life Balance.' Beyond the Rhetoric, J. Kodz, Institute for Employment Studies, 1/1/2002

Daniel J. Buysse. 'Treating Sleep Problems.' A Transdiagnostic Approach, Allison G. Harvey, Guilford Publications, 10/12/2017

Emma Sciberras. 'Sleep and ADHD.' An Evidence-Based Guide to Assessment and Treatment, Harriet Hiscock, Academic Press, 3/19/2019

Daniel Jackson. 'Digital Detox and Digital Minimalism.' Rockwood Publishing, 10/31/2023

Tanya Goodin. 'Off: Your Digital Detox for a Better Life.' Abrams, 3/13/2018

Bruce Headey. 'Health Cost Savings.' The Impact of Pets on Australian Health Budgets, Petcare Information and Advisory Service, 1/1/1995

Patricia McConnell, Ph.D.. 'The Other End of the Leash.' Why We Do What We Do Around Dogs, Random House Publishing Group, 2/19/200

Barrie Gunter. 'Pets and People.' The Psychology of Pet Ownership, Wiley, 6/2/1999

Courtney J. Bolstad. 'Dog Tired.' Examining the Relation Between Dog And/or Cat Ownership and Owners' Sleep, Mississippi State University, 1/1/2023

Ordóñez de Pablos, Patricia. 'Handbook of Research on Building Greener Economics and Adopting Digital Tools in the Era of Climate Change.' IGI Global, 6/24/2022

Doreen Kupke. 'Runtriz The Leader of mobile Hospitality.' Hotel Evolution, GRIN Verlag, 3/5/2013

Sharad Kumar Kulshreshtha. 'Post-COVID Tourism and Hospitality Dynamics.' Recovery, Revival, and Re-Start, Umendra Narayan Shukla, CRC Press, 1/9/2024

Alison Morrison. 'In Search of Hospitality.' Conrad Lashley, Routledge, 2/17/2010

Milton Kramer. 'Sleep and Mental Illness.' S. R. Pandi-Perumal, Cambridge University Press, 4/1/2010

Regina A. Shih. 'Sleep in the Military.' Promoting Healthy Sleep Among U.S. Servicemembers, Wendy M. Troxel, Rand Corporation, 4/30/2015

Jacqueline B. Marcus. 'Aging, Nutrition and Taste.' Nutrition, Food Science and Culinary Perspectives for Aging Tastefully, Academic Press, 4/15/2019

National Research Council. 'Sleep Needs, Patterns, and Difficulties of Adolescents.' Summary of a Workshop, Institute of Medicine, National Academies Press, 9/24/2000

William C. Dement. 'The Promise of Sleep.' A Pioneer in Sleep Medicine Explores the Vital Connection Between Health, Happiness, and a Good Night's Sleep, Random House Publishing Group, 3/7/2000

Teofilo Lee-Chiong, M.D.. 'Fundamentals of Sleep Technology.' Lippincott Williams & Wilkins, 6/1/2012

Sean P.A Drummond. 'Advances in the Psychobiology of Sleep and Circadian Rhythms.' Melinda L. Jackson, Taylor & Francis, 12/19/2023

Benjamin C. Parris. 'Vital Strife.' Sleep, Insomnia, and the Early Modern Ethics of Care, Cornell University Press, 8/15/2022

Alexander McCall Smith. 'Forensic Aspects of Sleep.' Colin M. Shapiro, John Wiley & Sons, 5/5/1997

Clarence Watson. 'Psychiatric Expert Testimony.' Emerging Applications, Kenneth J. Weiss, Oxford University Press, 1/1/2015

Herbert Hill. 'Black Labor and the American Legal System.' Race, Work, and the Law, Univ of Wisconsin Press, 1/1/1985

Ana C. Krieger. 'Social and Economic Dimensions of Sleep Disorders, An Issue of Sleep Medicine Clinics.' Elsevier Health Sciences, 2/7/2017

Yenni Payeski. 'Trouble sleeping?.' Evolve your spirituality, Tektime, 10/11/2022

Georg Feuerstein. 'Lucid Waking.' Mindfulness and the Spiritual Potential of Humanity, Inner Traditions / Bear & Co, 8/1/1997

Ray Giles. 'Sleep! the Secret of Greater Power and Achievement.' Literary Licensing, LLC, 8/1/2011

David J. Berghuis. 'The Addiction Treatment Planner.' Includes DSM-5 Updates, Robert R. Perkinson, John Wiley & Sons, 1/28/2014

Helen Rhodes Wallace. 'Sleep As The Great Opportunity Or Psychoma.' Literary Licensing, LLC, 3/1/2014

Desjarlais, Malinda. 'The Psychology and Dynamics Behind Social Media Interactions.' IGI Global, 7/26/2019

Sharon M. Weinstein. 'B is for Balance, Second Edition: A Nurse's Guide to Caring for Yourself at Work and at Home, 2015 AJN Award Recipient.' Sigma Theta Tau, 10/15/2014

George Everett Partridge. 'The Nervous Life.' Sturg & Walton Company, 1/1/1911

Yvette Green. 'Healthy Sleeping Habits: How to Adopt Healthy Sleeping Habits.' A Simple Guide to a Better and Healthy Sleeping Habit, Speedy Publishing LLC, 11/12/2014

Wendy M. Troxel. 'Sleep in the Military.' Promoting Healthy Sleep Among U.S. Servicemembers, Rand Corporation, 4/30/2015

Peter J. Kurz. 'Hypnosis in the Management of Sleep Disorders.' William C. Kohler, Taylor & Francis, 7/6/2017

Nathaniel Wallace. 'Scanning the Hypnoglyph.' Sleep in Modernist and Postmodern Representation, BRILL, 9/7/2016

Meir Kryger. 'Sleep in Art.' How Artists Portrayed Sleep and Dreams in the Last 7000 Years, Independently Published, 6/28/2019

Deirdre Barrett. 'The Committee of Sleep.' How Artists, Scientists, and Athletes Use Dreams for Creative Problem-solving-and how You Can, Too, Crown Publishers, 1/1/2001

Suzanne LeVert. 'The Pocket Idiot's Guide to a Good Night's Sleep.' Martin C. Moore-Ede, Alpha Books, 1/1/1999

Eleftherios Alamanos. 'The Role of Digital Technologies in Shaping the Post-Pandemic World.' 21st IFIP WG 6.11 Conference on e-Business, e-Services and e-Society, I3E 2022, Newcastle upon Tyne, UK, September 13–14, 2022, Proceedings, Savvas Papagiannidis, Springer Nature, 9/6/2022

Enrique G.. 'Sleep Deprivation Decoded: Worldwide Strategies, Tips, and Techniques for Better Rest.' Enrique Gérman, 6/1/2023

Maisy Collection. 'Fix Your Sleep Schedule.' 21 Days of Fixing Your Sleep Schedule, Independently Published, 7/5/2021

R. Robert Auger. 'Circadian Rhythm Sleep-Wake Disorders.' An Evidence-Based Guide for Clinicians and Investigators, Springer Nature, 5/26/2020

Pure Doxyk. 'Ubersleep: Nap-Based Sleep Schedules and the Polyphasic Lifestyle Second Edition.' Lulu.com, 6/15/2013

Michael Speca. 'Mindfulness-Based Cancer Recovery.' A Step-by-Step MBSR Approach to Help You Cope with Treatment and Reclaim Your Life, Linda Carlson, New Harbinger Publications, 2/3/2011

Stephan Bodian. 'Meditation For Dummies.' John Wiley & Sons, 3/3/2011

Miriam Z. Klipper. 'The Relaxation Response.' Herbert Benson, M.D., Harper Collins, 9/22/2009

Jon Kabat-Zinn. 'Meditation Is Not What You Think.' Mindfulness and Why It Is So Important, Hachette Books, 5/1/2018

Thomas Roth. 'Kryger's Principles and Practice of Sleep Medicine E-Book.' Meir H. Kryger, Elsevier Health Sciences, 12/16/2021

Carla Jungquist. 'Cognitive Behavioral Treatment of Insomnia.' A Session-by-Session Guide, Michael L. Perlis, Springer Science & Business Media, 6/2/2006

Yong-Ku Kim. 'Frontiers in Psychiatry.' Artificial Intelligence, Precision Medicine, and Other Paradigm Shifts, Springer Nature, 11/9/2019

Sheila Garland. 'Adapting Cognitive Behavioral Therapy for Insomnia.' Sara Nowakowski, Elsevier, 11/11/2021

Ranjot Singh Chahal. 'Why Sleep is Important: 5 Rules for Optimal Rest.' Rana Books Uk , 8/27/2023

Willow R. Stone. 'Stress Buster Tips To Help You Overcome Stress.' BornIncredible.com, 1/1/2023

Samantha Westwood. 'Stress No More!.' Your Personal Toolbox to Manage Stress, CreateSpace Independent Publishing Platform, 3/15/2017

Ethan D. Anderson. 'Sleep Well Tonight: Your Guide to Overcoming Insomnia.' BornIncredible.com, 1/1/2023

Christopher. 'Sweat, Sleep, Repeat.' Harnessing the Sleep Benefits of Exercise, Self, 11/4/2023

Devann O'Connell. 'Physical Activity and Sleep in Children with Down Syndrome.' Saint Joseph's University, 1/1/2017

Christina M. Jackson. 'Vitamin C.' Nutrition, Side Effects, and Supplements, Nova Science Publishers, Incorporated, 1/1/2011

Karman Meyer. 'Eat to Sleep.' What to Eat and When to Eat It for a Good Night's Sleep—Every Night, Simon and Schuster, 5/14/2019

Lan-Anh Le. 'Handbook of nutrition, diet and sleep.' Victor R. Preedy, Springer, 6/2/2013

Judith A. Owens. 'A Clinical Guide to Pediatric Sleep.' Diagnosis and Management of Sleep Problems, Jodi A. Mindell, Lippincott Williams & Wilkins, 1/1/2010

Thomas Roth. 'Principles and Practice of Sleep Medicine E-Book.' Expert Consult Premium Edition Enhanced Online Features, Meir H. Kryger, Elsevier Health Sciences, 11/1/2010

Aurora Brooks. 'The Ultimate Guide to Bedtime Routines: From Bath Time to Lullabies.' BabyDreamers.net, 9/8/2023

Alexandra Paige. '101 Ways to Lull Your Baby to Sleep.' Bedtime Rituals, Expert Advice, and Quick Fixes for Soothing Your Little One, Cider Mill Press, 11/1/2016

Davide M. Dominoni. 'Effects of Artificial Light at Night on Organisms: From Mechanisms to Function.' Alejandro Ariel Ríos-Chelén, Frontiers Media SA, 12/1/2022

James A. Bourgeois. 'On-Call Geriatric Psychiatry.' Handbook of Principles and Practice, Ana Hategan, Springer, 4/13/2016

LILY N. SINCLAIR.. 'The Ancient Wisdom of Acupuncture: Applying Traditional Principles to Modern Life.' Xspurts.com, 1/1/2023

Karen S. Schieman. 'Optimizing Sleep in the Intensive Care Unit, An Issue of Critical Care Nursing Clinics of North America , E-Book.' Optimizing Sleep in the Intensive Care Unit, An Issue of Critical Care Nursing Clinics of North America , E-Book, Elsevier Health Sciences, 5/31/2021

Diane C. Zelman. 'Healthy Sleep.' Your Questions Answered, John T. Peachey, Bloomsbury Publishing USA, 9/21/2023

P.J. Hauri. 'Case Studies in Insomnia.' Springer Science & Business Media, 8/31/1991

Mark Aloia. 'Behavioral Treatments for Sleep Disorders.' A Comprehensive Primer of Behavioral Sleep Medicine Interventions, Michael L. Perlis, Academic Press, 12/23/2010

Teofilo L. Lee-Chiong. 'Fundamentals of Sleep Technology.' Nic Butkov, Lippincott Williams & Wilkins, 1/1/2007

Charles A. Czeisler. 'Human Circadian Physiology.' Internal Organization of Temperature Sleep-wake and Neuroendocrine Rhythms Monitored in an Environment Free of Time Cues, Stanford University, 1/1/1978

William H. Moorcroft. 'Understanding Sleep and Dreaming.' Springer Science & Business Media, 3/25/2013

Board on Health Sciences Policy. 'Sleep Disorders and Sleep Deprivation.' An Unmet Public Health Problem, Institute of Medicine, National Academies Press, 10/13/2006

Donna Petersen. 'Foundations of Sleep Health.' F. Javier Nieto, Academic Press, 11/11/2021